MY SiDEWALKS ON
SCOTT FORESMAN
READING STREET
Intensive Reading Intervention

Practice
Book
Teacher's Manual

Level
C

Editorial Offices: Glenview, Illinois • Parsippany, New Jersey
New York, New York
Sales Offices: Boston, Massachusetts • Duluth, Georgia
Glenview, Illinois • Coppell, Texas • Sacramento, California • Mesa, Arizona

ISBN: 0-328-27224-8

4 5 6 7 8 9 10 V034 15 14 13 12 11 10 09 08 07
CC1

Contents

	Phonics	Comprehension	Vocabulary	Writing

UNIT 1 Dollars and Sense

	Phonics	Comprehension	Vocabulary	Writing
WEEK 1 Building a Community	1, 2	3	4	5
WEEK 2 Let's Make a Trade	6, 7	8	9	10
WEEK 3 Smart Saving	11, 12	13	14	15
WEEK 4 Money! Money!	16, 17	18	19	20
WEEK 5 Kid Business	21, 22	23	24	25

UNIT 2 Smart Solutions

	Phonics	Comprehension	Vocabulary	Writing
WEEK 1 Animal Answers	26, 27	28	29	30
WEEK 2 Good Choices	31, 32	33	34	35
WEEK 3 Brainstorms	36, 37	38	39	40
WEEK 4 Your Fair Share	41, 42	43	44	45
WEEK 5 Home Sweet Home	46, 47	48	49	50

UNIT 3 People and Nature

	Phonics	Comprehension	Vocabulary	Writing
WEEK 1 Green Thumbs in Action	51, 52	53	54	55
WEEK 2 Nature: The True Story	56, 57	58	59	60
WEEK 3 A Closer Look	61, 62	63	64	65
WEEK 4 To the Rescue!	66	67	68	69
WEEK 5 Dodging Disasters	70, 71	72	73	74

	Phonics	Comprehension	Vocabulary	Writing
UNIT 4 One of a Kind				
WEEK 1 Being Unique	75, 76	77	78	79
WEEK 2 From Top to Bottom	80, 81	82	83	84
WEEK 3 Hobbies	85, 86	87	88	89
WEEK 4 Being the First	90, 91	92	93	94
WEEK 5 People and Animals	95, 96	97	98	99
UNIT 5 Cultures				
WEEK 1 Dressing Up	100, 101	102	103	104
WEEK 2 Our World	105, 106	107	108	109
WEEK 3 Coming to America	110, 111	112	113	114
WEEK 4 Let's Eat!	115, 116	117	118	119
WEEK 5 Other Times, Other Places	120	121	122	123
UNIT 6 Freedom				
WEEK 1 American Symbols	124, 125	126	127	128
WEEK 2 Animal Freedom	129	130	131	132
WEEK 3 Expressing Yourself	133, 134	135	136	137
WEEK 4 It's the Law!	138	139	140	141
WEEK 5 Poetry	142	143	144	145

Name_____

Short *a*, *i*, and *o*

Directions Read each word. Look at the letter for the vowel sound.

l<u>a</u>mp

f<u>i</u>sh

l<u>o</u>ck

Directions Circle the word in each sentence with the same sound as *a* in *cap*. Then write the word on the line.

cat _____ **1.** The (cat) is Rob's pet.

map _____ **2.** The (map) is very big.

Directions Circle the word in each sentence with the same sound as *i* in *sip*. Then write the word on the line.

sit _____ **3.** I like to (sit) by the water.

trick _____ **4.** Their dog can do a (trick).

Directions Circle the word in each sentence with the same sound as *o* in *lot*. Then write the word on the line.

hot _____ **5.** The sun is very (hot).

sock _____ **6.** I found my (sock!)

clock _____ **7.** It is a very big (clock).

© Pearson Education C

Home Activity This page practices words with the short *a*, *i*, and *o* sounds as in *lamp*, *fish*, and *lock*. Work through the page with your child. Have your child make a collage of magazine pictures showing items that have short *a*, *i*, and *o* sounds. Help your child label each picture.

Phonics Short *a*, *i*, and *o*   **1**

Short *e* and *u*

Directions Read each word. Look at the letter for the vowel sound.

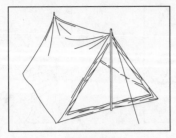

tent

drum

Directions Write two words that rhyme with each word below.

Possible answers given for 1–3:

1. bet <u>get, let, met, set</u> _____

2. pen <u>men, ten, when, then, den, hen</u> _____

3. bump <u>dump, pump, lump, jump, hump</u> _____

Directions Circle the word in each sentence with the same sound as the *e* in *then*. Then write the word on the line.

__let__ **4.** We (let) our dog run in the park.

__went__ **5.** We (went) to school.

__ten__ **6.** She got (ten) new hats.

Directions Circle the word in each sentence with the same sound as the *u* in *luck*. Then write the word on the line.

__such__ **7.** This is (such) a surprise!

__shut__ **8.** She (shut) the box.

__duck__ **9.** The (duck) swam across the pond.

School + Home

Home Activity This page practices the short *e* and *u* sounds as in *best* and *bump*. Work through the page with your child. Have your child write more short *e* and *u* words using the word parts *th*, *wh*, *ch*, and *ng* (*then, when, much, rung*) and use each word in a sentence.

© Pearson Education C

Name_____

Main Idea

- The **main idea** is the most important idea in a selection or a paragraph.
- The small pieces of information that tell about the main idea are the **supporting details**.

Directions Read the following passage. Then complete the Main Idea chart below.

Does your family have a pet? Cats are very good pets. They are so much fun! You will laugh when you watch them run and jump. They like to sit in your lap and let you pet them. They love it when you brush them. Cats don't have to go out when it is cold and wet. And when you are sad, they will give you a lot of love!

Main Idea Possible answers are given:
Cats are very good pets.

Supporting Details

| They are so much fun! You will laugh when you watch them run and jump. | They like to sit in your lap and let you pet them. | They do not have to go out when it is cold and wet. They will give you a lot of love! |

Home Activity This activity works with finding the main idea and supporting details. Tell your child about one of your favorite books. Ask your child to tell the main idea of what you told him or her and to identify the supporting details you gave.

Name_____

Vocabulary

Directions Choose a word from the box that best matches each definition. Write the word on the line.

Check the Words You Know

__build
__center
__city
__community

_center_____ **1.** a place people go to do things together

_community_____ **2.** a place where people live and work

_build_____ **3.** to put together

_city_____ **4.** a big community

Directions Write the word from the box that best completes each sentence. Write the word on the line.

_city_____ **5.** If you wanted to live with lots of people, you would move to a _____ .

_build_____ **6.** If you wanted a place to live, you would _____ a house.

_community_____ **7.** If you wanted to tell where your family lives and works, you would call it your _____ .

_center_____ **8.** If you wanted to know people, you would go to the community _____ .

Write an Ad

On a separate sheet of paper, write an ad for a community center in your neighborhood. Your ad should try to get people to come to the center. Use as many vocabulary words as possible.

© Pearson Education C

Home Activity This page helps your child learn to read and write the words *build, center, city,* and *community*. Work through the items with your child. Then ask your child to write the words and read them aloud.

Name_____

Writing

Directions Think about your community. Circle the words in each sentence that tell about your community. You may circle more than one in some sentences.

1. I live (in a city / in the country).

2. My community is (big / small / in between).

3. I like to (play / go to school) in my community.

4. My family (lives / works / shops) in my community.

5. The best thing about my community is (my friends / the community center / my school / the people).

Use your answers and other ideas to write several sentences about your community.

___Student responses will vary. Sentences should include some___

___specific information about the student's community.___

_____

_____

_____

_____

Home Activity This page helps your child think of how to complete a writing assignment telling about your community. Work through the page with your child. Discuss the answers your child circled.

Name_____

Long Vowels CVCe

Directions Add an *e* to the end of each word to make a new word. Write the new word on the line.

__tube_____ **1.** tub   __cane_____ **4.** can

__slide_____ **2.** slid   __hope_____ **5.** hop

__Pete_____ **3.** pet

Directions Circle the words that have the same vowel sound as the picture name.

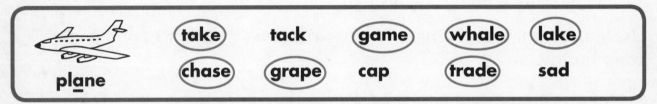

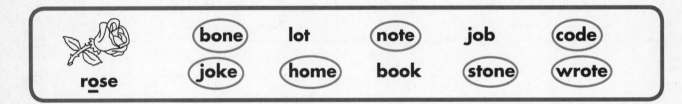

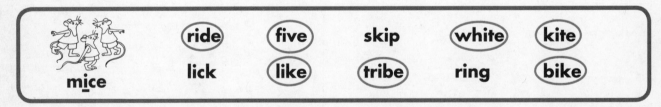

School + Home

Home Activity This page practices words with long vowel sounds in words such as *grade, these, kite, bone,* and *cute.* Work through the page with your child. Challenge your child to use each of the new words from items 1–5 in sentences. Have him or her identify the long vowel sound in each word.

© Pearson Education C

c/s/, g/j/, and s/z/

Directions Circle the word that names the picture.

cute   **(face)**

(cage)   big

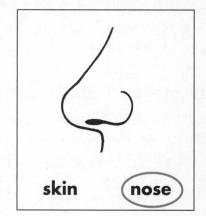

skin   **(nose)**

Directions Circle the words that have a sound like the c in *face*.

(race)   (nice)   cat   (rice)   come

(place)   tick   (cent)   (lace)   (fence)

Directions Circle the words that have a sound like the g in *gem*.

(orange)   goat   gum   (page)   thing

(age)   ago   (stage)   (huge)   good

Directions Circle the words that have a sound like the s in *use*.

(rose)   past   same   (hose)   (those)

(these)   said   (chose)   (his)   wish

Home Activity This page practices words that have the /s/ sound spelled *c* as in *race*, the /j/ sound spelled *g* as in *cage*, and the /z/ sound spelled *s* as in *rose*. Work through the page with your child. Have your child complete this sentence by changing the underscored items: *Face* is spelled with a *c* but it has the sound of an *s*.

© Pearson Education C

Sequence

- The **sequence** of a story is the order in which events happen.
- **Clue words**, such as *first*, *next*, and *then*, are often used to signal the sequence of events.

Directions Read the story. Then complete the diagram to tell what happened in the story.

Penny lives in the country. It is her job to get the eggs. First, she goes into the hen house and looks in the nests for eggs. She gets enough eggs. Then she goes back to her house. Finally, she puts the eggs away for her mother.

Title _____

1. Beginning

Penny goes into the hen house and looks in the nests for eggs.

⬇

2. Middle

When she has enough eggs, she goes back to her house.

⬇

3. End

Penny puts the eggs away for her mother.

4. Circle clue words in the story that tell the order of events. Then write them on the line below.

<u>First, Then, Finally</u>_____

Home Activity This page works with the order of events in a story. Work through the page together. Then have your child retell the story while acting out what happens.

© Pearson Education C

Name_____

Vocabulary

Directions Match each word with its definition. Write the word on the line.

___money___ **1.** the stuff used to buy things

___trade___ **2.** give something and get something

___goods___ **3.** things to buy

___worth___ **4.** what one thinks is its price

___swap___ **5.** another word for trade

Directions Write a word from the box to complete each sentence below.

6. Tom had some ___money___ to buy a bike.

7. The new bike was ___worth___ a lot of money.

8. First, he wanted to ___trade or swap___ his old bike for the new one.

9. Then he thought he would ___swap or trade___ several things with his friends.

10. Finally, Tom said he did not want to buy any of the ___goods___ .

Make a Poster

Imagine that your class is going to have a trade fair or a swap meet. Make a poster telling about it. Use as many of the vocabulary words as you can.

Home Activity This page helps your child learn to read and write the words *goods, money, swap, trade,* and *worth*. Work through the items with your child. Then ask your child to write the words and read them aloud.

Name_____

Writing

Directions Think about a trade you would like to make. Then follow the steps below. Responses will vary. An item should be circled in Steps 1, 2, and 3.

Step 1 Make a list of things you have to trade.

_____   _____
_____   _____
_____   _____

Step 2 Make a list of things you want to trade for.

_____   _____
_____   _____
_____   _____

Step 3 Make a list of people you might trade with.

_____   _____
_____   _____
_____   _____

Step 4 Go back to Step 1 and circle the thing you will trade.

Step 5 Go back to Step 2 and circle the thing you will trade for.

Step 6 Go back to Step 3 and circle the name of the person you will trade with.

On another sheet of paper, use your answers to write about a trade you would like to make. Be sure to tell why you want to trade.

Home Activity This page helps your child plan to write about a trade. Work through the page with your child. When your child finishes writing about a trade, listen to your child read the paragraph aloud.

Plurals and Inflected Endings -s, -es

Directions Add **-s** to each word. Write the new word on the line.

1. cat   __cats__
2. send   __sends__
3. ship   __ships__
4. frog   __frogs__
5. bump   __bumps__
6. bake   __bakes__
7. clam   __clams__
8. code   __codes__
9. cube   __cubes__

Directions Add **-es** to each word. Write the new word on the line.

10. box   __boxes__
11. kiss   __kisses__
12. dish   __dishes__
13. catch   __catches__
14. punch   __punches__
15. brush   __brushes__

Home Activity This page practices adding *-s* and *-es* to the end of words. Work through the items with your child. Write these words: *color, wish, word, glass.* Ask your child to add *-s* or *-es* to show more than one.

Endings -ed, -ing

Directions Add **-ed** and **-ing** to each word. Write the words on the lines.

Word	-ed	-ing
1. jump	jumped	jumping
2. ask	asked	asking
3. want	wanted	wanting
4. fill	filled	filling
5. learn	learned	learning
6. follow	followed	following
7. watch	watched	watching
8. listen	listened	listening
9. look	looked	looking
10. push	pushed	pushing
11. work	worked	working
12. pull	pulled	pulling
13. laugh	laughed	laughing
14. wash	washed	washing
15. remember	remembered	remembering

© Pearson Education C

Home Activity This page practices words with the endings *-ed* and *-ing*. Work through the items with your child. Write these words: *touch, cover, spill, print*. Ask your child to add *-ed* and *-ing* to each word and then say the new words.

Name_____

Sequence

- **Sequence** is the order in which events happen in a story.
- Look for these **clue words**: *first, next, then, finally.*
- As you read, **think about** what happens. This will help you keep track of the sequence of events.

Directions Read the passage.

Jim loves to draw pictures of a place in the country. First, he draws some grass in a big field. Next, he makes a big old house.

He makes a sun in the sky and colors it yellow. Then he draws some people and animals. Finally, he colors everything in the picture.

Directions Use the diagram to tell about the events of the story in the correct order.

First Jim draws some grass.

↓

Next He makes a house and sun.

↓

Then He draws some people and animals.

↓

Finally He colors everything in the picture.

© Pearson Education C

Home Activity This page allows your child to identify the sequence of events in a story. Name four events that happened in your family during the last year. Do not tell them in the order they happened. Ask your child to put them in the correct order. Encourage your child to use the words *first, next, then,* and *finally.*

Name_____

Vocabulary

Directions Draw a line from the word to its definition.

Check the Words You Know
__allowance   __expensive
__amount   __savings
__deposit

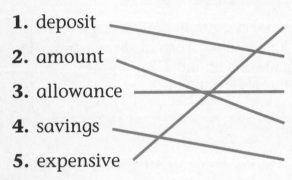

1. deposit — something put in a place to be kept safe

2. amount — the sum

3. allowance — a sum of money given to someone

4. savings — money saved

5. expensive — at a very big price

Directions Choose a word from the box that fits the meaning of the sentence. Write the word on the line.

6. Ali gets money for her __allowance__ .

7. She puts some of the money in the bank as __savings__ .

8. The money she puts in the bank is a __deposit__ .

9. Ali hopes to save a big __amount__ soon.

10. She wants to buy an __expensive__ game.

Write a Description

What could you do to earn money? On a separate paper, name some things you could do. Then tell which you would like best and why. Write at least three sentences. Use as many vocabulary words as you can.
Students may suggest doing extra chores around the house, walking a friend's dog, helping pick up trash in a neighbor's yard.

Home Activity This page helps your child read and write vocabulary words. Work through the items with your child. Then ask your child to read his or her description aloud.

© Pearson Education C

Name_____

Writing

Think about something you could save for. It should not be too expensive. Think about how you can get money and how much of it you can save.

Directions Finish the sentences below.

Responses will vary. Students' answers should be consistent with what they want to purchase.

1. I want to save to buy a _____ .

2. My allowance is $_____ .

3. I can save $_____ from my allowance.

4. I can get money by

_____

_____

_____

5. I think it will take _____ to save enough money.

6. Write a good first sentence. Tell what you want to buy.

_____

7. Write a good second sentence. Tell why you want it.

_____

On a separate paper, write about what you would buy and why. Be sure to tell how you would save enough money. Use the sentences you completed above to help you. Make sure all your words are spelled correctly.

Home Activity This page helps your child write about a topic. Work through the page with your child. Then have your child read the sentences aloud.

Name_____

Base Words and Endings -ed, -ing

Directions Add **-ed** and **-ing** to each word and write the new words. Remember to double the last consonant.

Word	-ed	-ing
1. stop	stopped	stopping
2. skim	skimmed	skimming
3. drop	dropped	dropping
4. swap	swapped	swapping
5. plan	planned	planning
6. grab	grabbed	grabbing
7. shop	shopped	shopping
8. hop	hopped	hopping
9. tug	tugged	tugging
10. beg	begged	begging
11. fill	filled	filling
12. hug	hugged	hugging

School + Home

Home Activity This page practices adding -ed and -ing to words. Work through the items with your child. Read a story with your child. Help him or her find words ending in -ed and -ing that double the last consonant before adding the ending.

Name_____

Base Words and Endings -ed, -ing

Directions Add **-ed** and **-ing** to each word and write the new words. Remember to drop the final **e**.

Word	-ed	-ing
1. race	raced	racing
2. hope	hoped	hoping
3. wipe	wiped	wiping
4. chase	chased	chasing
5. blame	blamed	blaming
6. trade	traded	trading
7. change	changed	changing
8. believe	believed	believing
9. like	liked	liking
10. use	used	using
11. move	moved	moving
12. promise	promised	promising

© Pearson Education C

Home Activity This page practices adding *-ed* and *-ing* to words. Work through the items with your child. Read a story with your child. Help him or her find words ending in *-ed* and *-ing* that follow the rule on this page.

Practice Book Unit 1   **Phonics** Base Words and Endings *-ed, -ing*   **17**

Compare and Contrast

- When you **compare** and **contrast**, you tell how two or more things are alike and different.

Directions Read the story. Then answer the questions below.

Teddy and Freddy are animals. They work and have fun. It is hot, and they need to make plans for the time when it gets cold. When it is cold, they can't find things to eat. They must find it now and save it.

Freddy looks for nuts. He puts them in a safe place. Then he goes to see his friends. Teddy looks for fun things to do. He spends a few minutes finding nuts. Freddy tells him to work. But Teddy doesn't listen. He likes to have fun!

When it is cold, Freddy has lots of nuts to eat. He is full. Teddy has nothing to eat. He has to ask Freddy to lend him something to eat. He promises to help next time.

How are Teddy and Freddy alike?

1. They are ___animals___ .

2. They ___work___ and have ___fun___ .

3. They must find ___something___ to eat and ___save___ it for the winter.

How are Teddy and Freddy different?

4. Freddy ___looks___ for nuts, but Teddy just has ___fun___ .

5. When it is cold, Freddy has ___something___ to eat, but Teddy has ___nothing___ .

6. Think of words to contrast Teddy and Freddy. Freddy ___works hard___ , but Teddy ___likes to play___ .

Home Activity This page helps your child compare and contrast. Work through the items with your child. Read an animal story or fable with your child. Ask him or her to compare and contrast two characters.

© Pearson Education C

Name_____

Vocabulary

Directions Solve each riddle with a word from the box. Write the word on the line.

1. I am 1¢.

What am I? __penny__

2. I am 25¢.

What am I? __quarter__

3. I am 100 cents.

What am I? __dollar__

4. I am 5 pennies.

What am I? __nickel__

5. I am a round piece of money.

What am I? __coin__

Directions Write the word from the box that fits the sentence on the line.

6. I used the __nickel__ to get the 5 cent picture.

7. I used the __quarter__ to get the 25 cent box.

8. I used the __dollar__ to get the 100 cent cap.

9. I used the __penny__ to get the 1 cent surprise.

10. A penny is a __coin__ .

Write a Story

Imagine that you have a coin collection. Write a story about your coins. Use as many vocabulary words as possible to describe the collection.

Home Activity This page helps your child read and write vocabulary words. Work through the items with your child. Then ask your child to read his or her story to you.

© Pearson Education C

Name_____

Writing

Directions Answer the questions to help you get ideas for your new money. **Responses will vary based on the kind of money each student creates.**

1. What is the name of your new money? You can give it your name. You can name it after a thing or place. You can name it after your cat, for example, Max Money. You can make up a new word.

_____

2. Is your money a coin or a bill?

_____

3. How many cents or dollars is it?

_____

4. What are some good ideas for pictures and colors for your money?

_____   _____

_____   _____

_____   _____

On another paper, draw your money. Draw the front and back. You may need to draw it more than once to get it perfect. Then write about your money. Tell its name, why you chose that name, and how much it is. Tell about the pictures on your coin or bill. Use vocabulary words. Be sure all your words are spelled correctly.

School + Home **Home Activity** This page helps your child design new money and describe it. Work through the page with your child. Ask your child to show you the picture and read the description aloud.

Name_____

Syllables VC/CV

Directions Circle the words in the box with a **short vowel** sound in **the first syllable.** Write the words on the lines.

afraid	become	(fossil)	(intend)	(object)	today
always	easy	(happen)	(invent)	people	(zigzag)

Order of answers 1–6 will vary.

1. fossil

2. happen

3. intend

4. invent

5. object

6. zigzag

Directions Choose a word from the box to complete each sentence. Write the word on the line.

ribbon	lesson	mitten	rabbit

rabbit _____ **7.** Ed's pet _____ is little.

mitten _____ **8.** Mary lost her _____ on the ice.

ribbon _____ **9.** The box had a _____ on it.

lesson _____ **10.** Today's _____ at school was about snakes.

© Pearson Education C

Home Activity This page practices words with short vowels in the first syllable. Work through the items with your child. Ask your child to write sentences about a kitten who went on a picnic.

Syllables VC/CV

Directions Circle each word that has a **short vowel** sound in the first syllable and a **long vowel** sound in the last syllable. Write the word on the line.

___tadpole___ **1.** A (tadpole) becomes a frog.

___reptile___ **2.** A snake is a (reptile).

___trombone___ **3.** I have a (trombone) for the school band.

___inhale___ **4.** You (inhale) through your nose.

___mistake___ **5.** I made one (mistake) on the math test.

Directions Circle the word in each row that has a **short vowel** sound in the first syllable and a **long vowel** sound in the last syllable.

6. (umpire)	boxes	promise
7. cover	(exhale)	minute
8. (admire)	question	color
9. woman	because	(engage)
10. either	stepping	(invite)

Home Activity This page practices words with short vowels and long vowels. Work through the items with your child. Ask your child to tell what letter stands for the short vowel sound in the words *tadpole* and *reptile*.

Name_____

Draw Conclusions

- A **conclusion** is a decision you make after you think about details and facts.
- Think about **what you already know** to draw a conclusion.

Directions Read the three details in the boxes. Then write a conclusion—what you think will happen.

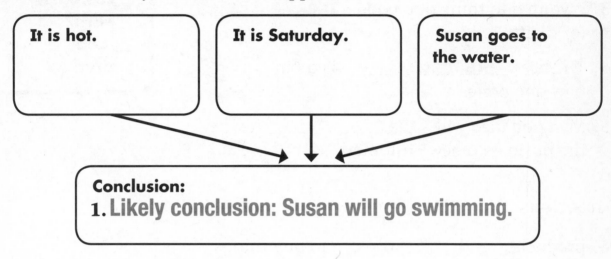

It is hot.

It is Saturday.

Susan goes to the water.

Conclusion:
1. Likely conclusion: Susan will go swimming.

Directions Read the conclusion. Then write one more detail that will help someone draw that conclusion.

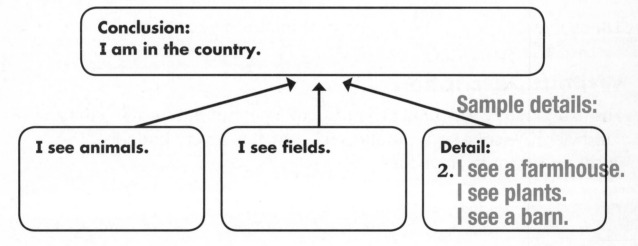

Conclusion:
I am in the country.

Sample details:

I see animals.

I see fields.

Detail:
2. I see a farmhouse.
I see plants.
I see a barn.

School + Home

Home Activity This page helps your child use details to draw a conclusion. Work through the items with your child. Read a story with your child. Stop now and then and ask your child to draw a conclusion about one of the characters.

Practice Book Unit 1

Comprehension Draw Conclusions **23**

Name_____

Vocabulary

Directions Fill in the blank with a word from the box that fits the meaning of the sentence.

1. The ___business___ sells things for pets.

2. One ___customer___ wants a gift for a dog.

3. I wanted to think of a good ___idea___ for a gift.

4. The best ___product___ is a big new dog bone.

5. My good idea will ___earn___ the business a new customer!

Directions Draw a line from the word to its definition.

6. product   a place to buy things

7. idea   to get money for work

8. earn   something that is made

9. customer   a person who buys things

10. business   a plan or thought in your head

Write a Description

Think of a really icky food product, like a peanut butter and jellyfish sandwich. Describe your product. Tell why it is a very bad idea. Use vocabulary words. Have fun!

Home Activity This page helps your child read and write vocabulary words. Work through the items with your child. Help your child think of other unusual food products and tell about the product and the business that would sell it.

Name_____

Writing

Directions Use the web below to list product ideas. Tell why they are good ideas. They can be serious—a cat box that cleans itself. Or they can be silly—magic soap you use one time and never have to take a bath again. You can put different topics in the web if you like.

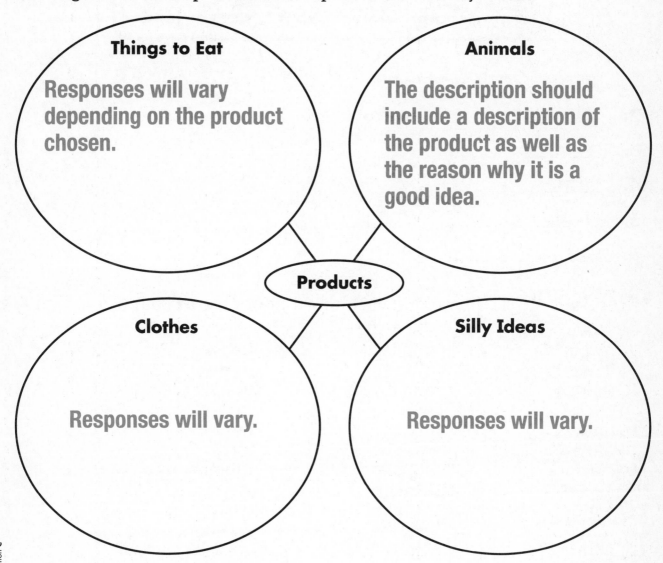

Things to Eat

Responses will vary depending on the product chosen.

Animals

The description should include a description of the product as well as the reason why it is a good idea.

Products

Clothes

Responses will vary.

Silly Ideas

Responses will vary.

Write a Description

On separate paper, list your ten best ideas. Draw a star by the very best idea. Describe the product and tell why it is a good idea. Tell who would buy it. Be sure all your words are spelled correctly.

Home Activity This page helps your child describe a product. Work through the page with your child. Ask your child to tell you about his or her second-best product idea.

Name_____

r-Controlled *ar*

Directions Circle the words in the box that have the sound **ar**. Write the words on the lines.

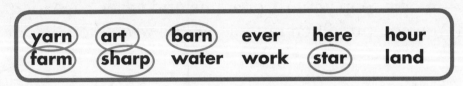

(yarn)	(art)	(barn)	ever	here	hour
(farm)	(sharp)	water	work	(star)	land

Order of answers 1–6 will vary.

1. yarn

2. art

3. barn

4. farm

5. sharp

6. star

Directions Circle the word in each row that has the **ar** sound.

7. (carpet)   rabbit   invent

8. lesson   mitten   (market)

9. father   (target)   button

10. (darling)   tadpole   umpire

11. reptile   (carton)   basket

12. admire   exhale   (garden)

© Pearson Education C

School + Home **Home Activity** This page practices words with *ar*. Work through the items with your child. Ask your child to name something in your home that is large, something that is sharp, and something someone bought at a market.

Name_____

r-Controlled *or, ore*

Directions Circle the word in each sentence that has **or** or **ore**.
Write the word on the line.

___fort___   **1.** I want to build a (fort) on a hill.

___born___   **2.** Peg was (born) in June.

___more___   **3.** Can I have some (more) water?

___store___   **4.** We buy things to eat at the (store.)

___North___   **5.** It is cold at the (North) Pole.

___corn___   **6.** We are eating (corn.)

___sports___   **7.** Leo likes to play (sports.)

___horse___   **8.** Bill can ride a (horse.)

Directions Underline the word in ( ) that has **or** or **ore**.
Then write the word on the line.

___popcorn___   **9.** We like to eat (apples, popcorn) at the movies.

___corner___   **10.** Janet lives around the (block, corner) from me.

___before___   **11.** When you count, 1 comes (after, before) 2.

___explore___   **12.** We like to (explore, play) in the park.

© Pearson Education C

Home Activity This page practices words with *or* and *ore*. Work through the items with your child. Ask your child to make up a silly sentence that uses these words: *corn, fork, horse.*

Name_____

Main Idea

- The **main idea** is what a story is all about.
- **Details** are small facts that help tell what the story is about.

Directions Read the story. Then answer the questions.

> Two pigs wanted to eat corn. They planted some seeds. They both watered the plants and watched the plants get bigger. They picked the corn together too.
>
> "We have too much corn," said Peter Pig.
>
> "We can give some corn to our friends," said Harry Hog.
>
> Their friends were thrilled. "You are smart farmers," said Cindy Cow. "You are very nice," said Sally Sheep. "You are good friends," said Gus Goat.
>
> After that, Peter and Harry planted corn every spring. When they picked the corn, they always gave some to their friends.

1. Circle the sentence that tells what the story is about.

> **Main Idea**
> Animals like to eat corn.
> (Two pigs give corn to their friends.)
> Corn needs water to get bigger.

Write details that help tell about the main idea.

Detail	**Detail**	**Detail**
2. Cindy Cow said:	**3.** Sally Sheep said:	**4.** Gus Goat said:
"You are smart farmers."	**"You are very nice."**	**"You are good friends."**

© Pearson Education C

Home Activity This page helps your child find the main idea and details in a story. Work through the items with your child. Ask your child to tell you about the lesson he or she learned from the story.

Name_____

Vocabulary

Directions Draw a line from the word to its definition.

1. environment   to save from harm or danger

2. adapt   to live through hard times

3. wildlife   everything that is around you

4. protect   wild animals and plants

5. survive   to change to fit different things

Check the Words You Know

__adapt
__environment
__protect
__survive
__wildlife

Directions Fill in the blank with the word from the box that fits the meaning of the sentence.

6. Some animals live in a cold __environment__ .

7. A fish cannot __survive__ out of water.

8. Rabbits are __wildlife__ that live in the country fields.

9. Mother animals work to __protect__ their young.

10. A big snake cannot change, or __adapt__ , to become a good pet.

Write an Advertisement

Choose an animal. Imagine that you are that animal. On a separate paper, write an ad about you! Tell why people should come see you at the zoo. Try to use vocabulary words.

Students should tell what is special or interesting about the animal they chose.

© Pearson Education C

School +Home

Home Activity This page helps your child read and write vocabulary words. Work through the items with your child. Ask your child to read his or her ad to you.

Name_____

Writing

Directions Plan what you will do. The questions below will help you. Write your ideas on the lines.

1. Choose an environment. It could be a hot, dry place; a cold place like the North Pole; or another place.

   Answers will vary.

2. What animals will you show?

   Answers will vary, but animals should be those found

   in the environment chosen.

   _____

3. What outdoor things are in the environment? Think about grass, plants, and water.

   Possible answers may include plants, land forms, bodies

   of water, depending upon the environment chosen.

4. How will you tell about your place on a poster?

   Possible response: I will use a title, labels, and captions.

5. How will you draw the environment? You can use crayons, markers, or paint. You also can cut out magazine pictures and put them on your poster.

   Answers will vary depending upon the environment chosen.

Make a Poster

Use a large sheet of paper to make a big poster. Draw your animals in their environment. Write sentences to tell how they adapt. Be sure your words are spelled correctly. **Posters should show the animals and plants in the environment the student chose.**

© Pearson Education C

Home Activity This page helps your child draw and write about animals and where they live. Work through the page with your child. Ask your child to tell you about the poster.

Name_____

Possessives

Directions Circle the possessive word in each sentence. Write the word on the line.

__frog's_____   **1.** The (frog's) skin is green.

__sister's_____   **2.** My (sister's) name is Beth.

__kids'_____   **3.** The (kids') room was a mess.

__brother's_____   **4.** Our (brother's) birthday is today.

__robins'_____   **5.** The (robins') nests are in trees.

__Fred's_____   **6.** (Fred's) cap is red and green.

__Earth's_____   **7.** The (Earth's) water is blue.

__dog's_____   **8.** Don't take my (dog's) bone!

__friend's_____   **9.** I looked at my (friend's) picture.

__mom's_____   **10.** My (mom's) cake smells good.

__Gus's_____   **11.** I will toss a stick to (Gus's) dog.

__father's_____   **12.** My (father's) idea was good.

__neighbors'_____   **13.** My (neighbors') cats are very large.

__family's_____   **14.** Our (family's) name is Miller.

__house's_____   **15.** The (house's) steps are wet.

© Pearson Education C

School + Home   **Home Activity** This page practices possessive words. Work through the items with your child. Read a story with your child. Ask him or her to point to words that are possessives.

Name_____

r-Controlled *er, ir, ur*

Directions Underline the word in each sentence with the sound **er** spelled **er.** Write the word on the line.

__germ__   **1.** A <u>germ</u> can make you sick.

__her__   **2.** Do you know <u>her</u> name?

__whisper__   **3.** Ken can <u>whisper</u>.

__lumber__   **4.** The house is made of <u>lumber</u>.

__cover__   **5.** That book has a robot on the <u>cover</u>.

Directions Underline the word in each sentence with the sound **er** spelled **ir.** Write the word on the line.

__first__   **6.** Tim is in <u>first</u> grade.

__third__   **7.** I am in <u>third</u> grade.

__twirls__   **8.** Mom <u>twirls</u> when we dance.

__girl__   **9.** This <u>girl</u> is my best friend.

__circus__   **10.** We sat in a tent at the <u>circus</u>.

Directions Underline the word in each sentence with the sound **er** spelled **ur.** Write the word on the line.

__turn__   **11.** It is my <u>turn</u> to tell a joke.

__curl__   **12.** The pig's tail has a <u>curl</u>.

__surf__   **13.** I like to swim in the <u>surf</u>.

__survive__   **14.** Fish can <u>survive</u> in the lake.

Home Activity This page practices words with the vowel sound er spelled er, ir, and ur. Work through the items with your child. Write this sentence and read it to your child: *You better not get butter on your mother's sweater.* Ask your child to say the words with the sound er.

© Pearson Education C

Name_____

Compare and Contrast

- When you **compare and contrast**, you tell how things are alike and different.
- You can use a **Venn diagram** to help you **compare and contrast**.

Directions Read the passage.

Frogs and fish are a lot alike, but they are not the same.

Frogs and fish can swim in the water. Both frogs and fish eat other animals. Both can be green.

Frogs live in the water and on land. Fish can live only in water.

Frogs have legs. They use legs to jump and swim. Fish have fins. They use their fins to swim.

Directions Finish the Venn diagram to compare and contrast frogs and fish. On the left side, tell things about frogs. On the right side, tell things about fish. In the middle, tell things that are the same about frogs and fish.

Frogs
1. live in the water and on land
2. have legs
3. use legs to jump and swim

Both
4. can swim in water
5. eat other animals
6. can be green

Fish
7. live only in water
8. have fins
9. use fins to swim

© Pearson Education C

Home Activity This page helps your child compare and contrast. Work through the items with your child. Then ask your child to compare and contrast two people in your family.

Name_____

Vocabulary

Directions Draw a line from the word to its definition.

1. advice — the act of deciding

2. decide — words about what should be done

3. problem — a hard question

4. decision — something picked out

5. choice — to choose something

Directions Fill in the blank with the word from the box that fits the meaning of the sentence.

6. You can ___**decide**___ to write a long letter or a short note.

7. It is a ___**problem**___ if your bike has a flat tire.

8. "Do not tell a lie" is good ___**advice**___ .

9. You have a ___**choice**___ of four quarters or one dollar.

10. Dad finally made a ___**decision**___ about buying a pet.

Write Advice

Pam got this letter:

Possible answer: You should tell your friend that you are sorry. Promise to help your friend with another problem or decision.

To Pam,

I have a problem. I promised to help my best friend sell tickets to the soccer game. But I forgot! Now my friend is mad at me. What should I do?

A Sorry Friend

What advice can Pam give to "A Sorry Friend"? Use vocabulary words.

© Pearson Education C

Home Activity This page helps your child read and write vocabulary words. Work through the items with your child. Then ask your child to read you his or her advice aloud.

Name_____

Writing

Directions Not all decisions are easy to make. You must be brave to make some decisions. Read each question. Write your answers on the lines.

1. How was Rosa Parks brave?

Student's answer should mention how Rosa Parks stood up for

her rights.

2. Do you think she was sorry that she did not get up for the man?

Student's answer should explain whether or not Rosa Parks was sorry.

3. What happened because of Rosa Parks's decision?

Student's answer should tell that people protested and a fair rule for

bus riders was made.

4. Was Curt brave when he did not invite Gertrude to his party?

Student's answer should explain that Curt was not brave for not

inviting Gertrude just because of other animals' comments.

5. Was Curt brave when he invited Gertrude?

Student's answer should explain that Curt was brave for inviting

Gertrude, helping solve the problem.

6. Write sentences that tell about Rosa Parks and Curt. Sentences
will vary.

Rosa Parks was brave because _____.

Curt was brave because _____.

On another paper, tell about how Rosa Parks and Curt were brave. Tell about their choices and how they felt later. Use vocabulary words. Check your spelling. Student's response should tell about the choices Rosa Parks and Curt had to make and how they each felt later.

© Pearson Education C

Home Activity This page helps your child write about decisions people make. Work through the page with your child. Then ask your child to tell about a time when it was not easy for him or her to make a decision.

Name_____

Endings -er, -est

Directions Add **-er** and **-est** to each word. Remember that you may have to double the last consonant. Write the words on the lines.

Word	-er	-est
1. soft	softer	softest
2. short	shorter	shortest
3. wild	wilder	wildest
4. new	newer	newest
5. warm	warmer	warmest
6. kind	kinder	kindest
7. soon	sooner	soonest
8. full	fuller	fullest
9. poor	poorer	poorest
10. young	younger	youngest
11. cold	colder	coldest
12. long	longer	longest
13. old	older	oldest
14. big	bigger	biggest
15. sad	sadder	saddest

© Pearson Education C

Home Activity This page practices words with the endings -er and -est. Work through the items with your child. Line up sets of three things that are different heights or lengths. Ask your child to say which item is big/bigger/biggest and long/longer/longest.

Name_____

Vowel Sounds of y

Directions Choose the word in ( ) with the **long i** sound for **y**.
Write the word on the line.

___my_____ **1.** Jane is (my, may) name.

___by_____ **2.** Our house is (boy, by) the park.

___cry_____ **3.** I (cry, city) when I get hurt.

___fly_____ **4.** Birds like to (fire, fly).

___try_____ **5.** We (try, toy) to spell all the words.

Directions Circle the words in the box with the **long e** sound for **y**.
Write the words on the lines.

away	buy	carry	enjoy	funny	happy
pretty	silly	sorry	today	penny	

Order of 6–12 will vary.

6. ___carry_____ **10.** ___silly_____

7. ___funny_____ **11.** ___sorry_____

8. ___happy_____ **12.** ___penny_____

9. ___pretty_____

© Pearson Education C

Home Activity This page practices words with the long *i* and long *e* sounds of *y*. Work through the items with your child. Ask your child to write a sentence that uses the word *try* and tells something he or she would like to do.

Name_____

Main Idea

- The **main idea** is what a story is all about.
- **Details** are small pieces of information about the main idea.

Directions Read the story. Then answer the questions.

"Oh, no!" said Lin. "Today is Mom's party. I forgot to buy her a card."

Lin decided to make a card. She wanted it to be special. She thought for a long time. Then she had an idea.

Lin took some red paper. In pencil, she wrote I LOVE YOU MOM! Then she got Mom's button box.

She used paste to put the buttons over her pencil lines.

Oh, no! All the buttons are gone, and MOM! is still in pencil.

Lin had another idea. She got peas from the kitchen. She used paste to put the peas over the last pencil lines.

Lin's mom said she loved the birthday card.

What is the main idea of the story? Write it in the box. Write three details that tell about the main idea.

Main Idea
1. Lin makes a card for her mom.

Details

2. Lin uses red paper.

3. Lin uses paste to put buttons on the words.

4. Lin uses paste to put peas on the word Mom.

© Pearson Education C

Home Activity This page helps your child practice finding the main idea and details in a story. Work through the items with your child. Ask your child if he or she thinks that Lin's ideas were good.

Name_____

Vocabulary

Directions Choose the vocabulary word from the box and write it next to its meaning.

Check the Words You Know

__fail
__invention
__puzzle
__solution
__solve

___fail_____ **1.** to not do something

___solution_____ **2.** the answer to a problem

___solve_____ **3.** to find the answer

___puzzle_____ **4.** a game with many small parts

___invention_____ **5.** a new thing that someone makes

Directions Each sentence has a word missing. Circle the word at the end of each sentence that fits the meaning. Then write the word on the line.

6. Can you ___solve_____ this problem for me?   (solve) fail

7. The ___solution_____ is the answer.   puzzle (solution)

8. Film is a good ___invention_____ .   (invention) solve

9. This ___puzzle_____ has too many parts!   (puzzle) solve

10. My idea for a robot will not ___fail_____ .   invention (fail)

What Do You Think?

Tad invented a machine that can wash a dog alone. You put your dog in the machine, and it washes the dog in five minutes. You do nothing! Write a review of Tad's invention. Tell if you think it is a good idea or a bad idea. Use as many vocabulary words as you can.

Answers will vary, but some students may say that it is a good solution because you won't get wet. Washing a dog can be messy. This invention makes it easy. Others may say it is not safe.

Home Activity This page helps your child read and write vocabulary words. Work through the items with your child. Ask your child to read his or her review out loud to you.

© Pearson Education C

Name_____

Writing

Directions With your partner, talk about problems that could be solved with inventions. List some of them here.

_____

_____

_____

Talk about how you could solve the problems. Choose a problem and write it in the Problem box. Then write ideas for how to solve it in the Solution box. Think of an invention.

> **Problem**
>
> **Answers will vary, but students should state a problem and a solution. Each student should give ideas for a solution.**

> **Solution**

© Pearson Education C

Use another paper to draw a picture of an invention. Use pencil first. Then go over your lines with color pencils or markers. Write sentences to tell about your invention. Check the spelling of all your words.

Home Activity This page helps your child describe a problem and a solution. Work through the page with your child. Then have your child read aloud his or her sentences about the invention.

Name_____

Base Words and Endings
-es, -ed, -er, -est

Directions Add **-es** and **-ed** to each word. Remember to change **y** to **i.**
Write the words on the lines.

Word	-es	-ed
1. try	tries	tried
2. cry	cries	cried
3. dry	dries	dried
4. worry	worries	worried
5. carry	carries	carried

Directions Add **-er** and **-est** to each word. Remember to change **y** to **i.**
Write the words on the lines.

Word	-er	-est
6. funny	funnier	funniest
7. happy	happier	happiest
8. muddy	muddier	muddiest
9. early	earlier	earliest
10. heavy	heavier	heaviest

© Pearson Education C

Home Activity This page practices words that end with *-es, -ed, -er,* and *-est.* Work through the items with your child. Write *bunny, puppy,* and *party.* Ask your child to add *-es* to each word and to write the new words.

Name_____

Consonant Blends

Directions Underline the consonant blend at the beginning or the end of each word. Then write the word on the line.

1. smi<u>l</u>e   <u>smile</u>

2. ju<u>mp</u>   <u>jump</u>

3. fir<u>st</u>   <u>first</u>

4. <u>st</u>ripe   <u>stripe</u>

5. mi<u>n</u>t   <u>mint</u>

6. <u>st</u>rip   <u>strip</u>

7. <u>br</u>ing   <u>bring</u>

Directions Choose the word in ( ) with a consonant blend to complete each sentence. Write the word on the line.

<u>splash</u>   **8.** I like to (splash, sit) in the lake.

<u>three</u>   **9.** We read a story about (nice, three) bears.

<u>stretch</u>   **10.** Can you (stretch, move) your arm up?

<u>strong</u>   **11.** You must be (tired, strong) to carry me!

<u>Scrub</u>   **12.** (Scrub, Put) your legs in the bath.

Home Activity This page practices words with consonant blends, such as *strip*, *smile*, *splash*, *jump*, and *scrub*. Work through the items with your child. Ask your child to say and write five words that end in *nd*.

Name_____

Sequence

- **Sequence** is the order in which things happen in a story.
- Look for **clue words** such as *first, second, next, then,* and *last.*

Directions Read the story.

> Liz's dog Buster ran in the mud. He was very dirty. He needed a bath.
>
> First, Liz got a big tub and the hose. Liz filled the tub with water. She got Buster's towel.
>
> Next, Liz called for Buster. But he would not come. Buster hates baths! Liz found Buster under her bed. She pulled Buster and made him get in the tub.
>
> Then Liz washed Buster all over. When the bath was finished, Buster started to shake himself dry—and Liz got all wet!
>
> Last, Liz had to get dry. Buster did not use the towel. Instead, Liz used Buster's towel.

Directions Write these sentences in the correct place on the chart.

- Buster hid under the bed.
- Liz got a big tub and a hose.

- Liz used Buster's towel.
- Liz washed Buster.

First
1. Liz got a big tub and a hose.

▼

Next
2. Buster hid under the bed.

▼

Then
3. Liz washed Buster.

▼

Last
4. Liz used Buster's towel.

Home Activity This page helps your child identify the sequence of events in a story. Work through the items with your child. Ask your child to put these bedtime activities in order: get into bed, turn off bedroom light, put on PJs, and brush teeth.

Practice Book Unit 2

Comprehension Sequence **43**

Name_____

Vocabulary

Directions Draw a line to match each word with a meaning for that word.

1. responsible   having pride in what you do

2. right   not right; bad

3. proud   something you must do

4. responsibility   good and correct

5. wrong   being in charge

Directions Write the word from the box that best completes each sentence.

__responsibility__   **6.** Taking care of a pet is a big _____ .

__wrong__   **7.** It is _____ to hit another person.

__proud__   **8.** Tim was _____ when he won the race.

__right__   **9.** Saying "please" and "thank you" are the _____ things to do.

__responsible__   **10.** Who is _____ for getting the papers?

Write a Story

Imagine that a student *did* take pet mice to school. On another paper, write about what happened. Use as many vocabulary words as you can.

Answers will vary, but students should tell about what happened when mice were brought to school.

Home Activity This page helps your child read and write vocabulary words. Work through the items with your child. Then ask your child to read his or her story to you.

Name_____

Writing

Some people are **not** responsible:

- They break promises.
- They make a mistake and don't admit it. Or they blame another person.
- They do not watch what they do.
- They do wrong things.

Directions Think about what a child would be like if he or she were **not** responsible. Write your answers to the questions below.

1. What are some things he or she would do? **Possible response:**

   <u>Lose things</u>   <u>Forget to feed and water</u> pets

   <u>Forget to turn appliances off</u>   <u>Forget homework</u>

2. What would happen because he or she was not responsible? For example, what would happen if the child spilled milk or did not give the dog water?

<u>Response should describe a time when a child is not responsible</u>

<u>and what happens as a result.</u>

_____

3. How would the child's family feel? How would his or her friends feel?

<u>Possible response: The child's family would probably feel</u>

<u>disappointed and irritated.</u>

4. How would the child feel about not being responsible?

<u>Possible response: The child would probably feel guilty for</u>
<u>disappointing others.</u>

On another paper, write a story about a character who is not responsible. Use as many vocabulary words as you can. Check the spelling of all your words.

Home Activity This page helps your child write a story. Work through the page with your child. Ask your child if he or she is responsible or is not responsible. Then have your child read his or her story to you.

© Pearson Education C

Name_____

Syllables VC/V and V/CV

Directions Circle the words in the box with a **short vowel** sound in the **first syllable.** Then write the words on the lines.

robot (body) (comet) (finish) frozen
(never) notice over hotel (travel)

1. __body__
2. __comet__
3. __finish__
4. __never__
5. __travel__

Directions Circle the words in the box with a **long vowel** sound in the **first syllable.** Then use the words to complete the sentences. Write each word on the line.

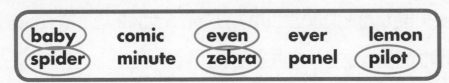

(baby) comic (even) ever lemon
(spider) minute (zebra) panel (pilot)

__pilot__   6. A _____ flies a plane.

__even__   7. Ten is an _____ number.

__baby__   8. The _____ cries a lot.

__zebra__   9. The _____ is black and white.

__spider__   10. A _____ has eight legs.

© Pearson Education C

School + Home   **Home Activity** This page practices words with short and long vowels in the first syllable. Work through the items with your child. Ask your child to use three of the words with a short vowel in the first syllable in sentences.

Name_____

Long a Spelled *ai, ay*

Directions Circle the word in ( ) with the **long a** sound. Then write the word on the line.

___play___ **1.** Winston always likes to ((play)/plan) soccer.

___say___ **2.** Remember to (slam/(say)) "thank you."

___wait___ **3.** Will you ((wait)/dance) for me after school?

___snail___ **4.** A (cat/(snail)) lives in a shell.

___train___ **5.** I take a ((train)/car) to visit my uncle.

___clay___ **6.** Mom made the pot with ((clay)/yarn).

Directions Circle the word with the **long a** sound. Then underline the letters that stand for that sound.

7. (del<u>ay</u>)   answer   among

8. cabin   father   (ok<u>ay</u>)

9. along   (det<u>ai</u>l)   animal

10. (r<u>ai</u>sin)   watch   alone

11. finally   (subw<u>ay</u>)   half

12. family   because   (cont<u>ai</u>n)

Home Activity This page practices words with long a spelled *ai* and *ay*. Work through the items with your child. Ask your child to collect some magazine pictures of things that have the long a sound in their names.

Name_____

Draw Conclusions

- A **conclusion** is a decision you arrive at after you think about what you read.
- You use **details** to help **draw a conclusion.**
- Think about **what you already know** to help you **draw a conclusion.**

Directions Read the story.

> Jon was going to the park to skate. He was going with his friend Sara. Before he went out, Jon put on his jacket. Then he put on his scarf and grabbed his gloves. Jon was almost out of the house when he heard his mother say his name. She was holding his hat!

Directions Complete the graphic organizer. Draw a conclusion by circling a sentence in the top box. In the bottom boxes, write details from the story that help you draw the best conclusion.

Conclusion
1. Jon's mother is mad at him.
   (It will be cold at the park.)
   Sara does not want to skate.

Possible answers:

Details

Detail
2. Jon puts on a jacket and scarf.

Detail
3. Jon gets his gloves.

Detail
4. Jon's mother will give him his hat.

© Pearson Education C

Home Activity This page helps your child draw conclusions. Work through the items with your child. Ask your child to read the story on the page again and draw a conclusion about what season it is—summer, fall, winter, or spring. Ask your child how he or she arrived at that conclusion.

Name_____

Vocabulary

Directions Choose the word from the box and write it next to its meaning.

__extreme__ **1.** much more than usual; very great

__weather__ **2.** the sun, wind, or rain in a certain place

__climate__ **3.** the kind of weather a place has

__shelter__ **4.** something that covers or protects

__protection__ **5.** act of keeping someone safe from harm

Directions Each sentence has a word missing. Circle the word at the end of each sentence that fits the meaning. Write it on the line.

6. The __weather__ today is cold and rainy. (weather) protection

7. A barn is a __shelter__ for animals. climate (shelter)

8. An umbrella gives __protection__ from rain. extreme (protection)

9. Florida has a warm and sunny __climate__ . (climate) shelter

10. A thunder storm is __extreme__ weather. protection (extreme)

Write About Climate

On another paper, write about the climate where you live. Is it often cold, hot, wet, dry, or just right? Write three sentences to describe the climate of the place where you live. Use vocabulary words. **Answers will vary, but students should write about the climate in their area.**

© Pearson Education C

Home Activity This page helps your child read and write vocabulary words. Work through the items with your child. Ask your child if he or she likes the climate where you live and to tell why or why not.

Name_____

Writing

Directions Choose a type of shelter that you would like to live in. You can use an idea from the box or another one you like better. Write your ideas on the lines.

1. I would like to live in a(n)

_____ .

Student should tell which type of shelter he or she would like to live in.

igloo (ice house)
tent
farm house
log cabin
big ship
house in the city
house in the country

2. List some good things about living in this shelter.

Student may list good things about

this shelter such as warmth, dryness.

3. What special things should you have in your shelter?

Student should tell what is needed to live in this shelter.

_____   _____

4. How is this shelter different from where you live now?

Student should explain how this shelter is different from his or

her home.

5. Who would live with you in this shelter?

Student should tell who would also be living in this shelter.

On another paper, describe your shelter. Tell what it looks like in your shelter. Tell what the land looks like around your shelter. Tell why it is fun to live there. Use vocabulary words. Check the spelling of all your words.

Answers will vary, but student should describe the shelter and include vocabulary words.

Home Activity This page helps your child write a description. Work through the page with your child. Then ask your child to read his or her description to you.

Name_____

Long e: e, ee, ea

Directions Circle the word in each sentence that has the same sound as the *e* in *he*. Write the word on the line.

_____She_____ **1.** (She) wants to plant roses in her garden.

_____be_____ **2.** Will you (be) coming to my school?

_____We_____ **3.** (We) are going to the park later today.

_____me_____ **4.** Tim is going to call (me) after school.

Directions Circle the word in each sentence that has the same sound as the *ee* in *heel*. Write the word on the line.

_____meet_____ **5.** Sam will (meet) Ann at her house to do homework.

_____wheel_____ **6.** The back (wheel) on my bike is flat!

_____feed_____ **7.** My sister forgot to (feed) the dog.

_____green_____ **8.** The (green) apples are the best.

Directions Circle the word in each sentence that has the same sound as the *ea* in *leaf*. Write the word on the line.

_____Each_____ **9.** (Each) student will take the test.

_____seats_____ **10.** There are four (seats) in the room.

_____reached_____ **11.** Kara (reached) for the book on my desk.

_____clean_____ **12.** I have to (clean) my room before dinner.

Home Activity This page practices words with the long *e* sound as in *me, bee,* and *tea*. Work through the page with your child. Help your child make a list of more words with the long *e* sound.

© Pearson Education C

Name_____

Contractions

Directions Use each pair of words to make a contraction. Write the contraction on the line.

I'll	**1.** I will	don't	**6.** do not
he's	**2.** he is	you'll	**7.** you will
let's	**3.** let us	what's	**8.** what is
we'll	**4.** we will	aren't	**9.** are not
isn't	**5.** is not	hasn't	**10.** has not

Directions Use the words in ( ) to make a contraction to complete each sentence. Write the contraction on the line.

Here's **11.** (Here is) the peach tree I planted last fall.

It's **12.** (It is) full of peaches that are almost ripe.

I'm **13.** (I am) going to pick them for my mother.

She's **14.** (She is) planning to make a peach pie.

can't **15.** I (can not) wait!

© Pearson Education C

School + Home **Home Activity** This page asks your child to form contractions. Ask your child to identify the contractions on this page that are formed with a word plus *not*. Then ask your child to think of other contractions that are formed with a word plus *not*, such as *doesn't*, *shouldn't*, and *couldn't*.

Name_____

Sequence

- **Sequence** is the order of the steps in a process.
- **Clue words**, such as *first*, *then*, *before*, *after*, and *finally*, can tell you when something should be done.

Directions Read the following passage. Then answer the questions below.

Growing plants from seeds is easy. First, find a warm, sunny spot inside. Then fill a very little pot with some dirt. Before you plant, read the seed packet to find out how deep to plant the seeds. Make a little hole in the dirt. Then put two or three seeds in the hole. After you've covered the seeds with dirt, put a little water in the pot. Check the pot each day to see if it needs more water. Finally, plant the plants outside in the garden when they are two or three inches tall.

1. What is the first step to grow a plant from seeds?

find a warm, sunny spot

2. What is the second step?

fill a little pot with dirt

3. What do you need to know before you plant the seeds?

how deep to plant the seeds

4. When should you first water the plant?

after you've covered the seeds with dirt

5. When should the plant be moved to the garden?

when it's two to three inches tall

Home Activity This page practices the sequence of steps in a process. Work through the page with your child. Find a recipe for a vegetable dish and help your child prepare it for a family dinner. Use clue words, such as *first*, *next*, and *then*, as you discuss the recipe with your child.

Vocabulary

Directions Match each word from the box with its meaning.
Write the word on the line.

grow **1.** to become bigger

vegetable **2.** the leaves, stems, or other parts of a plant that people eat

soil **3.** what you put a plant in

flower **4.** the part of a plant that has color

scatter **5.** to put about in different places

Directions Write the word from the box that best matches each clue below.

6. The plant had a yellow _flower_ .

7. We will _scatter_ the seeds in the yard.

8. The stem of this plant is a _vegetable_ .

9. The plant grows in black _soil_ .

10. Water and sun help the plant _grow_ .

Write a Story

Write a short story about a rabbit that grows vegetables in her garden.
Be sure to use as many vocabulary words as possible in your story.

© Pearson Education C

Home Activity This page helps your child learn to read and write the words *flower, grow, scatter, soil,* and *vegetable*. Work through the page with your child. Then ask your child to write sentences using each of the vocabulary words. Encourage him or her to write complete sentences.

Name_____

Writing

Directions First, think about a garden you would like to make. Would it be a vegetable, flower, or rock garden? Would it be on land or a floating garden? Write your choice in the center of the web. Then think about what is special about that garden. Write your ideas in the other circles.

Possible responses are given.

colors, plants, roses vines, flowers, soil (flower garden)

rocks, plants, soil, stones, flowers, vines, bushes, trees (rock garden)

Students should choose one type of garden.

beans, peas, corn plants, sticks, vines, soil (vegetable garden)

rocks, plants, fish, waterfalls, flowers (floating garden)

Students should write one characteristic of the garden in each outside oval.

Finally, on another sheet of paper, write three or four sentences about the garden you would like to make. Be sure to tell why it is special. Be sure to start each sentence with a capital letter and to end each sentence with a period.

Home Activity This page helps your child choose a topic to write about and organize the information about that topic. Work through the page with your child. After your child has written the sentences, ask him or her to read the paragraph aloud, listening for ways to improve it.

© Pearson Education C

Name_____

Long o: oa, ow

Directions Circle each word with the **long o** vowel sound as in *goal* and *snow*. Then write the word on the line.

toast	**1.** I will make (toast.)
yellow	**2.** The corn is (yellow.)
float	**3.** I can (float) in the water.
snow	**4.** We like to play in the (snow!)
soap	**5.** Wash the dog in (soap) and water.
show	**6.** I will (show) you a picture of my cat.
rainbow	**7.** I saw a (rainbow) after the storm.
bowl	**8.** There are apples in that (bowl.)
grow	**9.** You can (grow) plants in the garden.
know	**10.** Do you (know) how to ride a horse?

Directions Circle the word in each line with the **long o** vowel sound.

11. (goal)   among   torn

12. color   gone   (grown)

13. corn   won   (boast)

14. worst   (coating)   corner

15. (follow)   enjoy   money

Home Activity This page practices words with the long o vowel sound spelled *oa* and *ow*. Work through the items with your child. Ask your child to name the letters in the words in items 11–15 that stand for the long o sound.

© Pearson Education C

Name_____

Contractions 've, 're, 'd

Directions Use each pair of words to make a contraction. Write the contraction on the line. Remember to write an apostrophe (') to stand for missing letters.

1. I have ___I've___

2. you are ___you're___

3. they have ___they've___

4. you have ___you've___

5. they are ___they're___

6. I would ___I'd___

7. we have ___we've___

8. you would ___you'd___

9. they would ___they'd___

10. they have ___they've___

Directions Use the words in ( ) to make a contraction that completes each sentence. Write the contraction on the line.

___You're___ **11.** (You are) my best friend.

___she'd___ **12.** I asked my mom if (she would) bake cookies.

___We'd___ **13.** (We would) like to play in the park.

___we're___ **14.** On Saturday (we are) going to the zoo.

___he'd___ **15.** My brother said (he would) fix my bike.

© Pearson Education C

Home Activity This page practices contractions. Work through the items with your child. Ask your child to use the word *I'd* in a sentence to tell what he or she would like to do this weekend.

Name_____

Main Idea and Supporting Details

- The **main idea** is the most important idea about the topic.
- **Details** are small pieces of information about the main idea.

Directions Read the page from Tina's journal. Then complete the graphic organizer below.

April 12, 2006

Today our class went on a trip to the park by the school. We saw a bird's nest with eggs in it. Our teacher told us it was a robin's nest. We saw animals too—rabbits and ducks. We looked at lots of flowers too.

We hiked to the top of a hill. We sat on the grass in the sun to eat lunch. Some bugs got on me, but that was okay.

I was tired when I got home, but this was the best school trip ever!

Main Idea Possible responses are given:
1. This was the best school trip ever.

Supporting Details

2.

saw a bird's nest; saw rabbits;

3.

saw ducks; looked at flowers;

4.

hiked to top of hill; sat on grass and ate lunch

School + Home

Home Activity This page helps your child to identify the main idea and details in a passage. Work through the items with your child. Ask your child to read the journal entry again and find other details he or she didn't put in the chart.

Name_____

Vocabulary

Directions Fill in the blank with the word from the box that fits the meaning of the sentence.

1. People made up a ___myth___ to tell why there is thunder.

2. If you don't understand the question, the teacher will ___explain___ it.

3. Plants and animals are part of ___nature___ .

4. One kind of ___scientist___ studies the sky.

5. Maybe he will ___discover___ a new planet!

Directions Draw a line from the word to its definition.

6. nature   to see or learn of for the first time

7. discover   a story that tries to explain something in nature

8. scientist   the living things in the outside world

9. explain   to make plain or easy to understand

10. myth   a person who knows lots of science

Write an Interview

On another paper, write four questions you would like to ask a scientist who studies nature. Use as many vocabulary words as possible.

 Home Activity This page helps your child read and write vocabulary words. Work through the items with your child. Then ask your child to read his or her interview to you.

Name_____

Writing

Directions Think about nature and what would be fun to study. Look at the words in the box for ideas. Then answer the questions.

Responses will vary.

an animal	weather
a plant	a germ
the sky	the earth
the water	rocks

1. What would you want to study? **Students should choose what they want to study and answer the questions relating to their topics.**

2. Is your idea too big? You can't study animals because there are thousands of them. You would have to choose one. Write a smaller topic if yours was too big.

_____

3. What questions about your topic would you like to answer?

_____

_____

_____

4. Why do you think being a scientist would be fun?

_____

_____

_____

On another paper, write about being a scientist. Use your answers to the questions above to help you tell what you would like to explain and what you would hope to discover. Tell why you would enjoy it. Be sure all your words are spelled correctly. **Answers will vary.**

© Pearson Education C

Home Activity This page helps your child write about being a scientist. Work through the page with your child. Then ask your child to read his or her description to you.

Name_____

Compound Words

Directions Identify the two words that make up each compound word. Write the words on the lines.

1. __out__ + __side__ = outside

2. __sun__ + __shine__ = sunshine

3. __blue__ + __bird__ = bluebird

4. __sand__ + __box__ = sandbox

5. __class__ + __mate__ = classmate

6. __bath__ + __tub__ = bathtub

7. __butter__ + __fly__ = butterfly

8. __pine__ + __cone__ = pinecone

Directions Choose the compound word to complete each sentence. Write the word on the line. Draw a line between the two words that make up each compound word.

__sea|shell__   **9.** At the beach I found a (seashell/rock) on the sand.

__cat|fish__   **10.** For lunch, we cooked (tacos/catfish) on a fire.

__sun|shine__   **11.** The (sunshine/soil) helped the plants grow.

__Every|body__   **12.** (We/Everybody) had fun on our trip to the beach!

School + Home   **Home Activity** This page practices compound words. Work through the items with your child. Write the words *rowboat*, *spaceship*, and *inside*. Ask your child to say the words and draw a line between the two words that make each compound.

Name_____

Long *i*: *igh*, *ie*

Directions Circle each word with the **long *i*** sound. Then write the word on the line.

_flight_____ **1.** Fred took a (flight) in an airplane.

_pie_____ **2.** We ate peach (pie) at lunch.

_flies_____ **3.** The bird (flies) to the top of the tree.

_sight_____ **4.** A rainbow is a pretty (sight!)

_lie_____ **5.** It is fun to (lie) on the ground and look up at the stars.

_light_____ **6.** The lamp gave us lots of (light.)

Directions Circle the word with the **long *i*** sound. Then underline the letters in the circled word that stand for that sound.

7. coin   (tr<u>ie</u>d)   rain

8. (m<u>igh</u>t)   will   mitten

9. picnic   clip   (t<u>ie</u>d)

10. invent   (br<u>igh</u>t)   spill

11. girl   lived   (n<u>igh</u>t)

12. (cr<u>ie</u>d)   field   silly

School + Home **Home Activity** This page practices words with the long *i* sound spelled *igh* and *ie*. Work through the items with your child. Help your child write two sentences, one using the word *high* and one using *tie*.

Draw Conclusions

- A **conclusion** is a decision you reach after thinking about facts and details in what you read.
- You can use **what you already know** to help you draw a conclusion.
- Then **ask yourself,** "Does my conclusion make sense?"

Directions Read the passage. Then answer the questions.

Jeff was going to visit his grandmother. Jeff's mother took him to the store to get some new clothes for his trip. They also picked out something nice for Jeff to bring to his grandmother. That night, Jeff packed his bag with everything he needed for his trip the next day.

That morning, Jeff woke up very early. He went down to see if his mom was making something to eat. She was not there. It was very dark outside. He went back to his room and looked at the clock. It was two o'clock in the morning!

1. Where is Jeff going on his trip?

He is going to visit his grandmother.

2. Where does Jeff's mother take him?

She takes Jeff to the store to buy clothes and something for his grandmother.

3. What does Jeff do the night before his trip?

Jeff packs his bag with everything he needs for the trip.

4. What happens the morning of Jeff's trip?

Jeff wakes up and finds out that it is only two o'clock in the morning.

5. How does Jeff feel about visiting his grandmother? How can you tell?

Sample response: Jeff is very excited about his trip because he wakes up too early.

Home Activity This page helps your child draw conclusions. Work through the items with your child. Read a story with your child and have him or her draw a conclusion about a character in the story.

© Pearson Education C

Vocabulary

Directions Solve each riddle with a word from the box. Write the word on the line.

1. You use me when you eat something.

What am I? __taste__

2. You use me when you feel something.

What am I? __touch__

3. You use me when you see something.

What am I? __sight__

4. You have five of these to help you enjoy the world.

What are they? __senses__

5. I am another word for notice.

What am I? __observe__

Directions Draw a line from the word to its definition.

6. senses   sense used to know the flavor of things

7. touch   to see; to notice

8. observe   what sight, smell, hearing, taste, and touch are

9. sight   sense used to feel things

10. taste   sense used to see things

Write a Description

On another paper, tell which sense you like best: sight, touch, taste. Tell why it is your favorite. Give an example of you using that sense. Use vocabulary words in your answer.

© Pearson Education C

Home Activity This page helps your child read and write vocabulary words. Work through the items with your child. Ask your child to tell about something that smells good or something that tastes good.

Name_____

Writing

Think about a good place to be. It can be anywhere—the beach, a forest, a ball game, your room at home, or even the moon!

Directions Fill in the table with words that describe your place. You can use ideas from the box to help you. **Responses will vary depending on the place selected by the student. Students should tell how their senses help to describe their place.**

colors	sweet
shapes	soft
people	hard
animals	yummy

My Special Place	
1. What I see	
2. What I hear	
3. What I smell	
4. What I feel	
5. What I taste	

6. Write a good sentence to begin your description. It should tell what or where your place is.

_____

_____

7. Write a good second sentence.

I like my place because _____

_____ .

On another paper, describe your place. Tell about what you see, hear, smell, feel, and taste. Make sure your words are spelled correctly. **Answers will vary but should be sensory descriptions.**

Home Activity This page helps your child write a description. Work through the page with your child. Then have your child read the description aloud.

Syllables: Consonant + *le*

Directions Write the two syllables that make up each word on the lines.

1. __cud__ + __dle__ = cuddle
2. __waf__ + __fle__ = waffle
3. __smug__ + __gle__ = smuggle
4. __top__ + __ple__ = topple
5. __lit__ + __tle__ = little
6. __tram__ + __ple__ = trample
7. __han__ + __dle__ = handle
8. __sim__ + __ple__ = simple
9. __ta__ + __ble__ = table
10. __set__ + __tle__ = settle

Directions Choose the word in the box that matches each picture. Write the word on the line. Then draw a line to divide it into its syllables.

eagle
marble
puzzle
cattle
candle

11. __puz/zle__

12. __ea/gle__

13. __cat/tle__

14. __can/dle__

15. __mar/ble__

© Pearson Education C

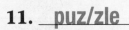

School + Home **Home Activity** This page practices words that have a final syllable made up of a consonant + *le*, such as *bugle*, *giggle*, and *purple*. Work through the page with your child. Then work together to think of words that rhyme with *middle*, *fable*, and *simple*. *(fiddle, riddle; able, cable, table; dimple)*

Draw Conclusions

- A **conclusion** is a decision you reach after you think about details and facts.
- As you read, think about the details and facts and **what you already know** to draw conclusions about what you read.

Directions Read the following passage. Then complete the diagram below to draw a conclusion about Jean. **Possible answers are given.**

> Jean worked very hard to train for the big race. She did not want to settle for last place. So she got up early every morning to run before school. Each day she ran a little faster. She also ran after school.
>
> Each day she could run a little bit longer. She made sure to eat well and get enough sleep. On the day of the race, Jean knew she was going to win.

Facts and Details

1. **Jean got up early every morning to run before school. She ran a little faster each day.**

↓

Facts and Details

2. **Jean ran after school. She ran a little longer each day.**

↓

Facts and Details

3. **Jean ate well and got enough rest.**

↓

Conclusion

4. **Jean may win the race because she has trained well.**

Home Activity This page practices drawing conclusions. Work through the page with your child. Ask your child to add to the story about Jean by coming up with other details that would support the conclusion he or she drew about the story.

Name_____

Vocabulary

Directions Match each word with its meaning. Write the word on the line.

__endangered__ **1.** in danger of no longer living or existing

__elephant__ **2.** a huge gray animal with a long trunk and tusks

__vanish__ **3.** to go out of sight; to be gone

__extinct__ **4.** no longer living or existing

__rescue__ **5.** to save from harm

Directions Write the word from the box that best completes each sentence.

6. Some animals are __endangered__ because of polluted water and air.

7. Others, like the __elephant__ , are hunted for their parts.

8. People and groups are coming to their __rescue__ .

9. They don't want these animals to __vanish__ from the Earth.

10. They are protecting these animals so that they do not become __extinct__ .

© Pearson Education C

Home Activity This page helps your child read and write vocabulary words. Work through the items with your child. Then ask your child to write sentences using each of the vocabulary words. Remind him or her to write complete sentences.

Name_____

Writing

Directions Read the problems below. Then think about a solution to each problem. Write your solutions in the solution boxes.

Problem
People and factories dump garbage into rivers and lakes. The garbage endangers animals.

↓

Solution
Answers will vary. Students should provide a realistic solution, such as pass laws banning dumping.

Problem
Elephants are killed for their tusks. People make things from the tusks and sell them for a lot of money.

↓

Solution
Answers will vary. Students should provide a realistic solution, such as arrest people who sell the things.

On another sheet of paper, write about what people in your community can do to help protect endangered animals. Use your ideas in the diagram. Be sure to start each sentence with a capital letter and end each sentence with a period.

Home Activity This page helps your child think of solutions to problems that are facing endangered animals. Work through the page with your child. Discuss your child's solutions to the problems.

© Pearson Education C

Name_____

Diphthongs *ou, ow* /ou/

Directions Circle the word with **ou** or **ow** that has the same vowel sound as **out**. Write the word on the line.

___Ouch___	**1.** Jan said, "Ouch!" when she fell on the ice.
___found___	**2.** I found two pennies in my pocket.
___brown___	**3.** My kitten has brown fur.
___clouds___	**4.** There are gray clouds in the sky.
___now___	**5.** I don't want to go to sleep now!
___growl___	**6.** Some animals growl when they are angry.
___flower___	**7.** A rose is my favorite flower.
___house___	**8.** Your house is across the street.
___ground___	**9.** There is ice on the ground.
___around___	**10.** Mary lives around the corner.

Directions Circle each word with the same vowel sound as the first word. Underline the letters that stand for the vowel sound.

11. around	enough	mound	touch
12. town	amount	you	bought
13. bounce	could	grow	howling
14. allow	thought	our	young
15. powder	surround	group	country

© Pearson Education C

Home Activity This page practices words with *ou* and *ow* with the vowel sound in *out*. Work through the items with your child. Ask your child to write this sentence: *I found a brown crayon on the ground.* Ask him or her to underline the letters that make the vowel sound in *out*.

Name_____

Suffixes -*ly*, -*ful*

Directions Add the suffix -**ly** or -**ful** to each base word. Write the new word on the line.

1. cheer   +   ful =   __cheerful__

2. nice   +   ly =   __nicely__

3. happy   +   ly =   __happily__

4. power   +   ful =   __powerful__

5. sad   +   ly =   __sadly__

6. thank   +   ful =   __thankful__

7. sudden +   ly =   __suddenly__

8. lucky   +   ly =   __luckily__

Directions Add -**ly** or -**ful** to the base word in ( ) to best complete each sentence. Write the new word on the line.

__careful__   **9.** Be (care) when you use scissors.

__quickly__   **10.** I ran (quick) in the race.

__colorful__   **11.** The flowers in the garden are (color).

__slowly__   **12.** A snail moves (slow).

 Home Activity This page practices words with the suffix -*ly* or -*ful*. Work through the items with your child. Say the words *wonder*, *wild*, *warm*, and *usual*. Ask your child to write new words with the suffix -*ly* or -*ful*.

© Pearson Education C

Name_____

Compare and Contrast

- When you **compare and contrast,** you tell how things are alike and different.
- You can use a **Venn diagram** to **compare and contrast.**

Directions Read the passage.

We used to live on the East Coast. There were many bad storms! The storms had strong winds and heavy rain. Sometimes we covered our windows so they wouldn't break. We worried a little about our house. We stayed inside until the bad weather was over. Sometimes, we got into our car and drove to a safer place.

Now we live on the West Coast. We have earthquakes here. The ground shakes. The windows rattle in our home. Sometimes cups and plates fall off the table! We worry a little about a big earthquake. We believe that our house will not fall down. We run outside to keep safe. But usually the earthquake is a small one.

Directions Use the words in the box to complete the Venn diagram.

> go outside   cover windows
> ground shakes   worry a little
> heavy rain   try to be safe
> windows rattle   strong winds
> stay inside   things fall off tables

Bad Storm
1. stay inside
2. heavy rain
3. cover windows
4. strong winds

Both
5. try to be safe
6. worry a little

Earthquake
7. go outside
8. ground shakes
9. windows rattle
10. things fall off tables

© Pearson Education C

Home Activity This page helps your child compare and contrast. Work through the items with your child. Ask your child to tell what happened during a recent storm or other bad weather.

Name_____

Vocabulary

Directions Write the word from the box that fits each sentence.

Check the Words You Know

__emergency
__flood
__hurricane
__natural
__warning

1. Rain and wind were part of the storm, a __hurricane__ .

2. There was so much water that we had a __flood__ .

3. We were ready because we heard a __warning__ on TV.

4. It is important to prepare for an __emergency__ .

5. Hurricanes and blizzards are __natural__ disasters.

Directions Draw a line from the word to its meaning.

6. hurricane — a sudden need to act

7. warning — a storm with strong winds and heavy rain

8. emergency — a great flow of water

9. flood — produced by nature

10. natural — advice given in advance

Write a Weather Report

A hurricane is coming! People need to know what will happen. On another paper, write a report that tells what the weather will be like. Tell about wind, rain, and floods. Use as many vocabulary words as you can.

Student's weather report should warn of a hurricane and say that there will be heavy rain, strong winds, and possible flooding.

© Pearson Education C

Home Activity This page helps your child read and write vocabulary words. Work through the items with your child. Then have your child read his or her weather report to you.

Name_____

Writing

Directions Think about an emergency. Think about what you and your family would need if you had to leave home. Use the web to help you make a plan. In the center oval, write the type of emergency. In each outside oval, list things you would take. You can change the topics in the ovals if you have better ideas.

Food
Possible responses: bottled water, juice or canned food items

Safety
cell phone, flashlight, radio, batteries

Kind of Emergency
hurricane, flood, tornado

For Fun
small games, cards, pen and paper

Other
blankets, towels, extra clothes, can opener

On another paper, tell what kind of emergency you chose. Then list the things you would take, one list for each topic. Next to each thing, you can tell which family member should bring it. You can't do all the work yourself!

Answers will vary, but students should tell what type of emergency was chosen, list things that are needed, and decide which family members are responsible for those items.

© Pearson Education C

Home Activity This page helps your child make an emergency plan. Work through the page with your child. Then consider a family meeting. Make plans for an emergency. Be sure everyone knows what to do.

Name_____

Diphthongs *oi, oy*

Directions Circle each word with **oi** or **oy** that has the same vowel sound as **toy**. Then write the word on the line.

coins_____   **1.** Kenny found a jar of (coins.)

boy_____   **2.** He had saved them when he was a little (boy.)

joyful_____   **3.** He felt (joyful.)

toy_____   **4.** Maybe now he could get the robot (toy.)

Choice_____   **5.** The "Your (Choice)" store sells robots.

voice_____   **6.** One robot had a loud (voice.)

noise_____   **7.** It made a beeping (noise.)

joined_____   **8.** Kenny (joined) his sister at the table.

enjoy_____   **9.** He told her he would (enjoy) the robot.

pointed_____   **10.** She (pointed) to the jar.

coins_____   **11.** To spend the (coins) would be bad.

spoil_____   **12.** It could (spoil) the set that they had.

Home Activity This page practices words with the *oy* sound heard in *toy* and *boil*. Work through the items with your child. Help your child write and talk about words with the vowel sound in *toy* or *boil*, such as *boy, joy, enjoy, annoy, foil, moist, toil,* and *loyal.*

Name_____

Prefixes *un-*, *re-*

Directions Add the prefix **un-** or **re-** to each base word. Write the new word on the line.

1. un-   +   lock   =   <u>unlock</u>

2. re-   +   fill   =   <u>refill</u>

3. un-   +   like   =   <u>unlike</u>

4. re-   +   draw =   <u>redraw</u>

Directions Write the word from the box that best fits each definition.

<u>redo</u>   **5.** to do again

<u>unsafe</u>   **6.** not safe

<u>rewrite</u>   **7.** to write again

<u>uncommon</u>   **8.** not common

> **uncommon**
> **rewrite**
> **redo**
> **unsafe**

Directions Add the prefix **un-** or **re-** to the word in ( ) to complete each sentence. Write the new word on the line.

<u>unload</u>   **9.** It is time to (load) the truck.

<u>redraw</u>   **10.** I will (draw) part of my picture.

© Pearson Education C

School + Home **Home Activity** This page practices words with the prefixes *un-* (unlock) and *re-* (replay). Work through the items with your child. Help your child to choose words from the box above and use them in sentences.

Name_____

Sequence

- **Sequence** is the order in a story—what happens first, next, and last.
- Sometimes **clue words** can tell you what happens *first, next,* and *last.*

Directions Read this passage. Then answer the questions below.

Lin had a plan to win the race. She would not run her fastest at the beginning. If she ran the whole race at top speed, she would be tired. Let the other girls get tired! Then Lin could run very fast and win. The sound of a horn started the race. At first, speedy Carla ran quickly and led the runners. Then Carla slowed down about halfway around the track. That is when Lin pushed herself to run faster. She passed two other runners. Next she passed Carla. Carla tried to catch up. Near the finish line, Carla was getting close. Lin felt her legs move even faster. Finally she crossed the line and won.

1. Did Lin have her plan before the race or when the race had started?

Lin had her plan before the race.

2. Who was the first runner to lead the race?

Carla was the first runner to lead the race.

3. What did Lin do when the leader slowed down?

Lin pushed herself to run faster.

4. What did Carla do when Lin began running faster?

Carla tried to catch up.

5. What clue word tells you that Lin's winning was the last part of the race?

Finally

© Pearson Education C

Home Activity This page allows your child to identify a sequence of events in a story. Work through the items with your child. Then ask your child to help you make up another story about a race and tell what happens first, next, and last.

Name_____

Vocabulary

Check the Words You Know

__audience	__perform
__famous	__talent
__instrument	__unique

Directions Fill in the blank with the word that fits the meaning of the sentence. Write the word on the line.

1. What is your special __talent__ ?

2. Do you play music in your own __unique__ way?

3. What __instrument__ do you know how to play?

4. Do you ever __perform__ in a show?

5. Who is in your __audience__ , besides your family?

6. Maybe some day you will become a __famous__ movie star.

Directions Draw a line from each word to its meaning.

7. instrument   having lots of fans

8. audience   one of a kind

9. famous   something used to make sounds

10. unique   people gathered to hear or see something

Write an Advertisement

On a separate sheet of paper, write an ad for someone with a unique talent who performs for others. Use as many of the vocabulary words as you can.

© Pearson Education C

Home Activity This page helps your child read and write vocabulary words. Work through the items with your child. Then have your child tell what the vocabulary words used in the ad mean.

Name_____

Writing

Directions Describe a musical instrument.
You can tell what the instrument looks like
and how it sounds.

What kind of instrument will you describe?

strings	brass	drum
bow	tune	strum
beat	voice	hum
twang	chime	honk
noise	piping	joyful

_____

1. Circle any words from the box that can help describe the instrument.

2. Write other words that you can use to describe the instrument or
   how it sounds.

_____

Now write ideas to use in your description.

3. What does the instrument look like?

_____

4. How does the instrument sound?

_____

5. Why do you like this instrument?

_____

**Answers will vary.
Descriptions should
include information
about the instrument,
its sound, and why it
was chosen.**

6. Write a good sentence that you might use to begin your description.

_____

On another paper, write your description. Identify the instrument and
describe it. Tell why you like it. Make sure you use capital letters and
punctuation correctly.

Home Activity This page helps your child write a description. Work through the page with your child. Then
have your child read the description aloud.

Name _____

Vowels *oo* in *moon*

Directions Circle the words in the box that have the same sound as the **oo** in **moon**. Then write the words on the lines.

four   ⟨too⟩
⟨noon⟩   ⟨soon⟩
⟨shoot⟩   took
boat   look
good   ⟨zoo⟩

1. __noon__

2. __shoot__

3. __too__

4. __soon__

5. __zoo__

Directions Write the new words on the line.

6. Change the *c* in *cool* to *sch*.

   What is the new word? __school__

7. Change the *b* in *boot* to *r*.

   What is the new word? __root__

8. Change the *l* in *loose* to *m*.

   What is the new word? __moose__

9. Change the *d* in *food* to *l*.

   What is the new word? __fool__

10. Change the *t* in *tool* to *st*.

    What is the new word? __stool__

© Pearson Education C

Home Activity This page practices words with the sound of *oo* as in *moon*. Play a rhyming game with your child. Ask him or her to give rhyming words for *moon*, *room*, and *pool*.

Name _____

Silent Consonants *kn, gn, mb*

Directions Read the story. Underline the words with the silent consonants **mb**, **kn**, and **gn.** Then write the underlined words on the lines.

CLASS
MEETS HERE

The sign on the knob said, "Class Meets Here." Maria wanted to learn to knit. She knew it would be fun. She knocked and she went in. Maria learned how to tie a knot in the yarn. Then she learned how to use her thumb to move the yarn. The yarn is as soft as a lamb. Maria was going to make a pair of knee socks. She worked hard until her fingers were numb.

1. sign
2. knob
3. knit
4. knew
5. knocked
6. knot
7. thumb
8. lamb
9. knee
10. numb

Directions Read each word. Underline the silent consonants. Then write the word.

11. gnat _____ gnat
12. crumb _____ crumb
13. know _____ know
14. thumb _____ thumb
15. gnome _____ gnome

School + Home

Home Activity This page practices words with silent consonants. Work through the items with your child. Use a dictionary and help your child name additional words that start with *kn* and *gn*.

Name _____

Compare and Contrast

- When you **compare and contrast,** you tell how things are alike and how they are different.
- You can use a **Venn diagram** to **compare and contrast.**
- Reading slowly helps you **notice details, key words, or other clues** the author uses in **comparing** and **contrasting.**

Directions Read the following passage. Then complete the diagram to compare and contrast what you read. Use these words: *paint, dance, slide, swings, school, race.*

Linda and Nan live on the same street. They like to go to school together. They often do different things. Linda likes to paint pictures. Nan likes to dance. When school is over, Linda and Nan play at the park. Nan likes to play on the slide. Linda likes to play on the swings. Both of the girls like to race around the path in the park.

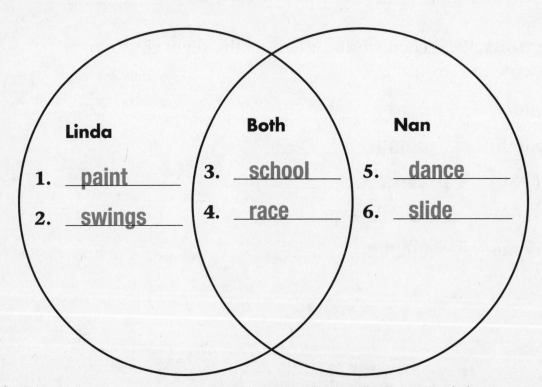

Linda

1. paint
2. swings

Both

3. school
4. race

Nan

5. dance
6. slide

© Pearson Education C

Home Activity The page helps your child compare and contrast the things two girls do. Draw a Venn diagram together. Write "Playing Outside" in the first circle, "Playing Inside" in the second circle, and "Both" where the two circles overlap. Ask your child to use the diagram to list games they play outside and inside and in both places.

Name _____

Vocabulary

Directions Solve each riddle with a word from the box. Write the word on the line.

1. I tell how high something is.

   What am I? __height__

2. I tell how deep something is.

   What am I? __depth__

3. I am the top of a very high hill.

   What am I? __summit__

4. I am another word for climb.

   What am I? __scale__

5. I am the highest point at the top of the very high hill.

   What am I? __peak__

Directions Write the word from the box that best completes each sentence below.

6. Marcus is going to __scale__ Mount Logan.

7. It is over 5,000 feet in __height__.

8. He cannot see its __peak__.

9. It will be a long climb to the __summit__.

10. Marcus gets himself into __position__ and begins to climb.

© Pearson Education C

Home Activity The page helps your child read and write vocabulary words. Ask your child to use this week's vocabulary words in sentences.

Name _____

Writing

Directions Think of questions for an interview. Write ideas on the lines.

1. Do you plan to interview a mountain climber or a free diver? Write your answer on the line.

<u>Answers 1–4 will vary.</u> _____

2. Circle the words that describe what you want to know.

age	practice	clothes	name	school
training	tools	place	lessons	feelings

3. Make a list of other things you'd like to know.

_____

_____

_____

_____

4. Most questions begin with the words *who, what, when, where,* and *how.* Circle the three words you will use in your questions.

who   what   when   where   how

5. Write three questions to use in the interview. Be sure to use a question mark at the end of each question.

<u>Questions will vary but should begin with the words circled in</u>

<u>item 4 and end with a question mark.</u> _____

_____

_____

_____

© Pearson Education C

Home Activity This page helps your child write questions for an interview. Work through the page with your child. Then have your child write three questions to ask you about your work or your favorite type of recreation.

Name _____

Vowel Patterns *ew, ue*

Directions Circle the word with **ew** or **ue** in each sentence. Then write the word on the line.

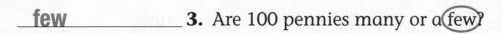

_____new_____ **1.** Roy got a (new) jacket for school.

_____blue_____ **2.** Jane used a (blue) crayon to draw a river.

_____few_____ **3.** Are 100 pennies many or a (few)?

_____stew_____ **4.** The (stew) has meat in it.

_____threw_____ **5.** Bob (threw) the toy to his dog.

_____glue_____ **6.** I used (glue) to put pictures on the page.

Directions Circle the word with **ew** or **ue**.

7. (clue)   laugh   people

8. draw   (crew)   heavy

9. (true)   money   you're

10. though   eight   (blue)

11. world   (dew)   found

12. woman   usual   (knew)

© Pearson Education C

School + Home   **Home Activity** This page practices words with the vowel patterns *ew* and *ue*. Work through the items with your child. Ask your child to name as many things as possible that are blue.

Name _____

Silent Consonants *st, wr*

Directions Choose the word in ( ) with the silent consonant, as in **st** or **wr,** to complete each sentence. Write the word on the line.

__wreck_____ **1.** Be careful! Don't (wreck, crack) the window.

__write_____ **2.** I want to (tell, write) a story about a dog that can fly.

__listening_____ **3.** Pat is (listening, dancing) to the music.

__glistening_____ **4.** The snow is (melting, glistening) in the sun.

__wrist_____ **5.** You wear a watch on your (leg, wrist).

__castle_____ **6.** The king and queen lived in a (castle, house).

Directions Circle each word in the box that has a silent consonant, as in **st** or **wr.** Write the circled words on the lines below.

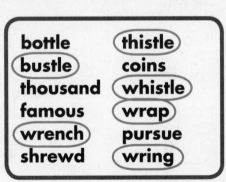

bottle	⟨thistle⟩
⟨bustle⟩	coins
thousand	⟨whistle⟩
famous	⟨wrap⟩
⟨wrench⟩	pursue
shrewd	⟨wring⟩

Order of words for 7–12 will vary.

st

7. __bustle_____

8. __thistle_____

9. __whistle_____

wr

10. __wrap_____

11. __wrench_____

12. __wring_____

© Pearson Education C

Home Activity This page practices words with the silent consonants *st* and *wr*. Work through the items with your child. Ask your child to write a sentence using the word *whistle*, and then read the sentence aloud.

Name _____

Draw Conclusions

- A **conclusion** is a decision you reach after thinking about what you read.
- You use **what you already know** to help you draw a conclusion.
- You **ask yourself,** "Does my conclusion make sense?"

Directions Read the following passage. Then answer the questions below. **Possible responses are given.**

> **M**y friends and I started a nature-writing club. We asked our parents to join us.
>
> We hiked in a different state park every week. We saw lakes, rivers, and streams. We saw leafy trees, green grasses, and flowers. We saw insects, birds, frogs, turtles, and small mammals. Sometimes, Mike went fishing, but no one else did.
>
> While we were there, we wrote about what we saw. After we had been to ten parks, we put our writing together to make a book.

1. Why do you think these friends wanted to start a nature-writing club?

They like to be outdoors. They like to write.

2. Why did they invite their parents to join them?

Their parents could take them to parks that are far away.

3. What do you think they wrote about?

They wrote about the plants and animals they saw.

4. Who most likely wrote about what it's like to go fishing? Explain.

Mike wrote about fishing. He was the only person who fished.

5. Write a question about the book the club members made. Then draw a conclusion to answer your question.

Did your book have pictures? I think it probably had pictures

because it helps tell about an animal if you show what it looks like.

Home Activity This page allows your child to draw conclusions. Work through the items with your child. Ask your child if he or she thinks the writing club members hiked in the winter or summer and explain why.

Name _____

Vocabulary

Directions Write the vocabulary word from the box next to its meaning.

__delight_____ **1.** great joy

__rare_____ **2.** hardly ever seen, found, or happening

__collection_____ **3.** a group of things that go together

__interest_____ **4.** a feeling of wanting to know or share in

__unusual_____ **5.** not common

__special_____ **6.** more than usual; different from others

> **Check the Words You Know**
>
> __collection
> __delight
> __interest
> __rare
> __special
> __unusual

Directions Write the word from the box that fits in each sentence.

7. Bea has a __collection_____ of many different plants.

8. She has an __interest_____ in things from nature.

9. It is a joy, or __delight_____, to find a new plant.

10. Some of her plants are common, but others are __unusual_____.

Write a Description

On a separate paper, write about something fun to collect. Tell why. Use as many of the vocabulary words as you can.

Students' descriptions should describe the collection and tell what is fun and/or interesting about it.

© Pearson Education C

Home Activity This page helps your child read and write vocabulary words. Work through the items with your child. Ask your child to circle the vocabulary words in his or her description and tell what they mean.

Name _____

Writing

Think about a hobby you have or a hobby that you would enjoy. Think of words to make the hobby sound like fun.

Directions Circle any words from the box that you can use to describe your hobby.

Now answer these questions.

delight	unusual
interest	unique
exciting	collection

1. What is the hobby?

Students should name the hobby.

2. How did you learn to do it?

Students should tell how they learned about the hobby.

3. What do you like best about the hobby?

Students should tell what is the most fun about the hobby.

4. Would your friends enjoy this hobby too? Explain.

Students should tell why the hobby is fun for anyone, or why it matches his or her unique interests.

5. Write a good sentence to begin your description.

Students should write an attention-grabbing first sentence.

On another paper, write about your hobby. Tell why you like it. Make sure your words are spelled correctly.

Home Activity This page helps your child write a description. Work through the page with your child. Then have your child read the description aloud.

© Pearson Education C

Name _____

Vowels *oo* in *foot*, *u* in *put*

Directions Circle each word with the vowel sound in **foot** and **put**.
Then write the word on the line.

_stood_____ **1.** Ben (stood) up when it was his turn to read.

_took_____ **2.** I (took) a trip to the beach.

_full_____ **3.** The glass is (full) of milk.

_wood_____ **4.** Our desks are made of (wood).

_Look_____ **5.** (Look) for the box under the bed.

_hood_____ **6.** Lin's jacket has a (hood) to keep her warm.

Directions Circle the words in the box that have the vowel sound in **foot**
and **put.** Write the words on the lines below.

7. _book_____
8. _cookie_____
9. _foot_____
10. _good_____
11. _pull_____
12. _wool_____

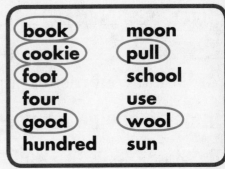

(book)	moon
(cookie)	(pull)
(foot)	school
four	use
(good)	(wool)
hundred	sun

© Pearson Education C

Home Activity This page practices words with the vowel sound in *foot* and *put*. Work through the page with your child. Ask your child to say one sentence using the word *pudding* and another sentence using the word *hook*.

Name _____

Suffixes -ness, -less

Directions Add the suffix **-ness** or **-less** to each word. Write the new word on the line.

1. pain + -less = __painless__
2. bold + -ness = __boldness__
3. end + -less = __endless__
4. fair + -ness = __fairness__
5. care + -less = __careless__
6. happy + -ness = __happiness__
7. worth + -less = __worthless__
8. good + -ness = __goodness__

Directions Add **-less** or **-ness** to the word in ( ) to complete each sentence. Write the new word on the line.

harmless
illness
sadness
useless

__illness__   9. You stay home from school when you have an (ill).

__harmless__   10. Most spiders are (harm). They won't hurt you.

__useless__   11. A nail without a point is (use).

__sadness__   12. Sue felt (sad) when her friend moved away.

© Pearson Education C

School + Home **Home Activity** This page practices words with the suffixes -ness and -less. Work through the page with your child. Ask your child to do something that shows silliness and then write a sentence to tell what he or she did.

Name _____

Compare and Contrast

- When you **compare and contrast**, you tell how things are alike and how they are different.
- You can use a **Venn diagram** to **compare and contrast**.

Directions Complete the Venn diagram to compare and contrast. Use the words from the box to compare the two games.

make a home run	**team of 11**
make a goal	**use a ball**
team of 9	**hit hard**
kick hard	**run fast**

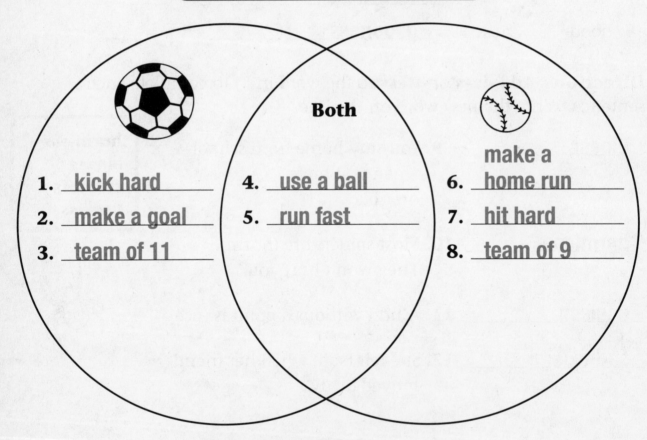

Both

1. kick hard
2. make a goal
3. team of 11

4. use a ball
5. run fast

make a
6. home run
7. hit hard
8. team of 9

Order of answers may vary.

Home Activity This page helps your child compare and contrast two games. Work through the page with your child. Draw a Venn diagram. Label the parts "Snow," "Both," and "Rain." Help your child complete the diagram.

© Pearson Education C

Name _____

Vocabulary

Directions Write the vocabulary word from the box next to its meaning.

waterfall   **1.** a place where water falls from a high place

attempt   **2.** a try; an effort

distance   **3.** the space in between

remarkable   **4.** worthy of notice; unusual

adventure   **5.** an unusual or thrilling journey

impossible   **6.** not able to be or happen

> **Check the Words You Know**
>
> __adventure
> __attempt
> __distance
> __impossible
> __remarkable
> __waterfall

Directions Write the word from the box that best fits the meaning of the sentence.

7. It is a long __distance__ from Earth to the moon.

8. Taking a raft down the river would be a thrilling __adventure__!

9. You can get wet if you stand near a __waterfall__ .

10. I made an __attempt__ to stand on my head, but I fell!

Write a Description

On a separate paper, write about an adventure you would like to have. Use as many of the vocabulary words as you can.

Possible answer: I would like to go to Pluto. It is a long _distance_ away. It would be an exciting _adventure_. I hope there are _waterfalls_ on Pluto!

© Pearson Education C

Home Activity This page helps your child read and write vocabulary words. Work through the items with your child. Ask your child if the adventure he or she wrote about is possible or impossible and tell why.

Name _____

Writing

A world record is something you do first or something you do best. Think about what would be fun to do.

Directions

1. Circle any words from the box that you might use.

2. Use the web to help you. Write your world record idea in the center oval. In the outside ovals, write words or phrases that tell about the world record.

On another paper, write a paragraph about your world record and how you would set it. Make sure your words are spelled correctly.

biggest
highest
longest
fastest
surprising
adventure
outstanding

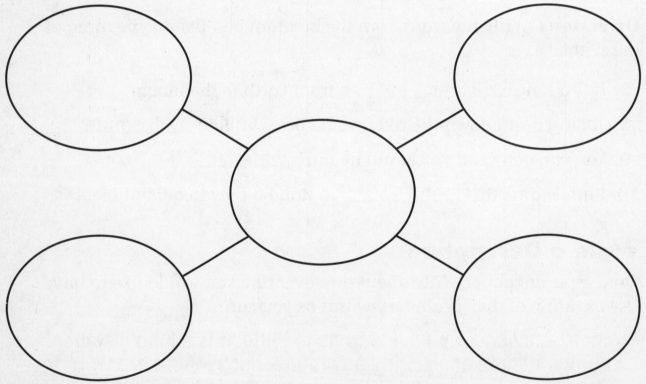

Students will likely want to make something big, long, or tall. They should use adjectives and verbs to describe the record and how they would accomplish it.

Home Activity This page helps your child write about a world record. Work through the page with your child. Then have your child read the paragraph aloud.

© Pearson Education C

Name _____

Short e: ea

Directions Choose the word in each group with the **short e** sound spelled **ea**. Write the word on the line.

___spread___   **1.** clean   spread   each

___weather___   **2.** search   greed   weather

___death___   **3.** freeze   beach   death

___instead___   **4.** instead   teach   preach

___steady___   **5.** reaching   steady   screeching

___deaf___   **6.** deaf   pioneer   creature

> bread
> head
> sweater
> thread

Directions Choose a word from the box that names the picture. Be sure the word you choose has the **short e** sound spelled **ea**.

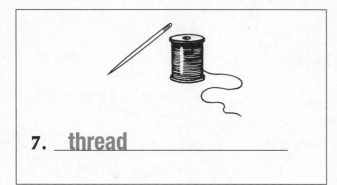

7. ___thread___

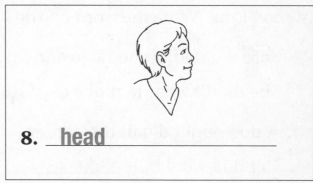

8. ___head___

9. ___sweater___

10. ___bread___

School + Home   **Home Activity** This page practices words with the short *e* sound spelled *ea* as in *bread*. Work through the page with your child. Have your child write five sentences using words from this page with the short *e* sound spelled *ea*.

Name _____

Prefixes *mis-*, *dis-*

- A **prefix** is a syllable added to the beginning of a word. Prefixes can help you figure out the meaning of a word you don't know.
- The **prefix** *dis-* means "the opposite of" or "not."
- The **prefix** *mis-* means "bad or badly" or "wrong or wrongly."

Directions Match the word with its meaning.

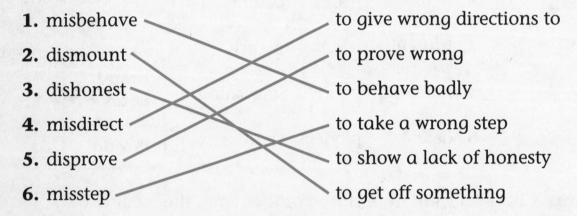

1. misbehave — to give wrong directions to

2. dismount — to prove wrong

3. dishonest — to behave badly

4. misdirect — to take a wrong step

5. disprove — to show a lack of honesty

6. misstep — to get off something

Directions Read each pair of sentences. Circle the word that belongs in the blank. Write the word on the line.

7. Sara wanted to choose just the right pet.

   She didn't want to make a ___mistake___ . (mistake) discontent

8. A dog might dig in the garden.

   Her dad would ___dislike___ that.   misfile (dislike)

9. A cat might scratch the chairs.

   That would ___displease___ her mother.   misplace (displease)

10. A bird might fly out of its cage.

   The family would ___mistrust___ such a pet. (mistrust) dismiss

© Pearson Education C

School + Home

Home Activity Your child forms and writes words with the prefixes *dis-* and *mis-* on this page. Work through the page with your child. Then ask your child to write sentences using the words with the prefixes *dis-* and *mis-* in items 1–6.

Name _____

Main Idea

- The **main idea** is the most important idea in a selection or a paragraph.
- The small pieces of information that tell about the main idea are the **supporting details.**

Directions Read the following passage. Then answer the questions below.

A cat uses its tail to tell people how it feels. A tail that moves back and forth very quickly means that the cat is angry. A tail that slowly moves back and forth means that the cat is happy. A tail tucked between the cat's legs means that the cat is worried. A tail held low to the ground with its hairs fluffed out means that the cat is afraid. And a tail held straight up and still means, "I'm glad to see you." So, if you want to know how a cat is feeling, watch its tail!

1. What is the main idea of the passage? **Possible answers are given.**

Cats use their tails to show their feelings.

2. What is one detail that supports the main idea?

An angry cat moves its tail back and forth rapidly.

3. What is another detail that supports the main idea?

A happy cat moves its tail slowly back and forth.

4. What might be a fact you think has been left out of this passage?

Answers will vary.

5. How do you think the writer knows about how cats use their tails?

The writer has spent a lot of time watching cats and what they do.

© Pearson Education C

Home Activity The activity on this page focuses on the main idea and supporting details. Find a newspaper or magazine advertisement for a product that is being sold in a store. Help your child decide what the ad is about and what the facts are about the product.

Name _____

Vocabulary

Directions Match each word with its meaning. Write the word on the line.

___adult___ **1.** a living thing grown to full size

___opportunity___ **2.** a good chance

___mimic___ **3.** to copy closely, to imitate

___adjust___ **4.** to change to make fit

___realize___ **5.** to understand clearly

___communicate___ **6.** to give or listen to information

Directions Write the word from the box that best completes each sentence below.

7. Seahorses are really fishes that

___mimic___ very tiny horses.

8. Mates do a greeting dance to

___communicate___ with each other.

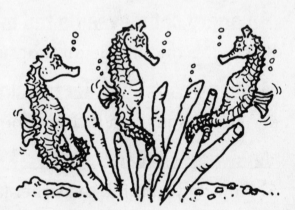

9. Baby seahorses must take care of

themselves and ___adjust___

to their surroundings.

10. Most ___adult___ seahorses

only live to be three years old.

© Pearson Education C

Home Activity This activity helps your child read and write vocabulary words. Ask your child to create a short story. Encourage him or her to use as many vocabulary words as possible.

Practice Book Unit 4

Name _____

Writing

Directions Think about what you can learn by studying animals. Answer the following questions.

1. Where can you study animals? Check each place where you might study animals.

_____ in zoos _____ in parks

_____ in backyards _____ on farms

_____ in homes _____ at school

2. What kinds of animals would you see? List two or three animals for each place.

in zoos _____ Responses should include a choice of _____

in backyards _____ places to study animals, what animals _____

in homes _____ would be found in that location, what the _____

in parks _____ animals might be doing, and what the child _____

on farms _____ could learn by studying the animals. _____

at school _____

3. What could you see the animals doing? Check each activity you might see.

_____ sleeping _____ playing

_____ eating _____ fighting

_____ running _____ discovering

_____ climbing _____ watching you

On a separate paper, write your answer to the question about what we can learn by studying animals. Make sure you use complete sentences.

Home Activity This page helps your child think of a topic to write about related to studying animals. Watch an animal in your home, outside, or on TV for a few minutes with your child and then discuss what you've observed and what it might mean.

Name_____

Vowel Sound in *ball:* a, al

Directions Choose the word with the vowel sound in *ball*. Write the word on the line.

small _____ **1.** We live in a (little, small) house.

also _____ **2.** My uncle lives with us (also, too).

talk _____ **3.** Sometimes we (speak, talk) about getting a bigger home.

almost _____ **4.** We (almost, around) decided to get a different house.

always _____ **5.** We are (always, still) glad that we stayed here.

call _____ **6.** This is the place we (sing, call) home.

Directions Write **al** to complete each word. Use the words in the box to help you. Write the whole word on the line.

| walk chalk fall halt tall wall |

fall _____ **7.** Don't f **a l** l on the ice!

chalk _____ **8.** You can write with ch **a l** k.

tall _____ **9.** The roof is very t **a l** l.

wall _____ **10.** The side of a room is a w **a l** l.

walk _____ **11.** We w **a l** k by the park on our way to school.

halt _____ **12.** The word h **a l** t means stop.

© Pearson Education C

Home Activity This page practices words that have the vowel sound in *ball*. Work through the page with your child. Ask your child to find a wall, a hall, and something tall in your home.

Name_____

Consonants *ph* /f/, *dge* /j/

Directions Choose the word from the box that matches each word below. Write the missing letters to complete each word. Say each word.

phone	phony
photo	trophy
graph	

1. tro <u>p</u> <u>h</u> y

2. <u>p</u> <u>h</u> o t o

3. g r a <u>p</u> <u>h</u>

4. <u>p</u> <u>h</u> o n y

5. <u>p</u> <u>h</u> o n e

trophy

photo

Directions Circle the word that has the *j* sound heard in *jar* or *edge*. Underline the letters that spell the *j* sound.

6. (ju<u>dge</u>)   guess   zigzag
7. grade   (fu<u>dge</u>)   north
8. graph   snail   (ri<u>dge</u>)
9. (we<u>dge</u>)   peach   ouch
10. night   (le<u>dge</u>)   giggle
11. cowboy   build   (bri<u>dge</u>)
12. (ba<u>dge</u>)   wrap   knife

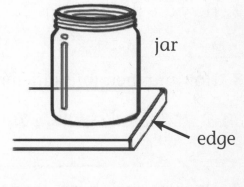

jar

edge

badge

bridge

Home Activity This page practices words that have the *f* and *j* sounds spelled *ph* and *dge*. Work through the page with your child. One at a time, say the words *lodge*, *phase*, *pledge*, and *phony*. Ask your child to make a fist if he or she hears the *f* sound and to jump if he or she hears the *j* sound.

© Pearson Education C

Name_____

Compare and Contrast

• To **compare and contrast** is to tell how things are alike and different.

Directions Read the following passage. Then answer the questions below.

> Don's dog is white with brown spots. Its fur is soft. It has a long tail. Pete's dog is black. It has soft fur. Its tail is short. Both dogs have loud barks! They both like to play catch, too.

1. How are the colors of Don's dog and Pete's dog different?

The exact wording of the students' answers will vary.

Don's dog is white with brown spots. Pete's dog is black.

2. How are the two dogs' fur alike?

Both dogs have soft fur.

3. How are their tails different?

Don's dog's tail is long. Pete's dog has a short tail.

_____

4. How are their barks the same?

Both barks are loud.

5. Both dogs like to catch a ball. Does this show a way they are alike or different? Tell how you know.

This shows how they are alike. The sentence says both.

_____

© Pearson Education C

Home Activity This page is about comparing and contrasting. Name your child's two favorite sandwiches. Talk about how they are alike and different.

Name_____

Vocabulary

Directions Draw a line to match each word with its definition.

1. custom — things to put on, like shirts

2. ordinary — ten years of time

3. tradition — a special way that people dress

4. decade — not special; common; everyday

5. clothing — the handing down of customs

6. style — a common way of doing something

Directions Write the word from the box that answers each question.

7. What is ten years?

   decade

8. What do you put on?

   clothing

9. What is a word for something that is not special?

   ordinary

10. What is something that many people do again and again?

    custom

Home Activity This page helps your child read and write vocabulary words. Work through the items with your child. Then help your child think of customs in your family.

Name_____

Writing

Think about the clothing you wear when it is cold. Compare and contrast it with the clothing you wear when it is hot.

Directions Write a paragraph about what people wear when it is hot outside. Also tell what people wear when it is cold outside.

same	**jeans**	**clothing**
different	**top**	**mittens**
coat	**scarf**	**shorts**
shirt	**boots**	

1. Circle any words from the box that you might use.

2. What can you wear on hot and cold days?

Accept reasonable responses. For example:

I can wear a shirt and jeans on hot or cold days.

3. What would you wear only on hot days?

Sample answer: I would wear shorts on hot days.

_____

4. Write two things you need when it is cold.

Sample answer: When it is cold, I need a coat and a hat.

_____

5. Write a good sentence to begin your paragraph.

Sentences can compare and contrast clothing for cold and hot

weather.

On another paper, write your paragraph. Compare and contrast clothes for hot days and cold days. Make sure your words are spelled correctly.

© Pearson Education C

Home Activity This page helps your child write sentences about a topic. Work through the page with your child. Then have your child read the paragraph aloud.

Name_____

Vowel Sound in *ball: au, aw*

Directions Choose the word in each group with the vowel sound in **ball**. Write the word on the line.

__law_____ **1.** law   farm   act

__pause_____ **2.** mad   pause   want

__haul_____ **3.** take   place   haul

__hawk_____ **4.** hawk   parents   class

__yawn_____ **5.** wrap   yawn   start

__auto_____ **6.** auto   day   hard

draw

Directions Write **au** or **aw** to complete each word. Use the word box to help you. Write the whole word on the line to the left.

> awful   because   straw   draw   lawn   saw

__saw_____ **7.** I s_aw_ a new book I wanted to read.

__because_____ **8.** I wanted to read it bec_au_se it was about horses.

__straw_____ **9.** The horses eat hay and sleep on str_aw_ .

__draw_____ **10.** I think I will dr_aw_ a picture of a horse.

__lawn_____ **11.** The horse can stand on the l_aw_n by the barn.

__awful_____ **12.** I hope my picture does not look _aw_ful.

© Pearson Education C

Name_____

Suffixes -er, -or

Directions Add the suffix to each base word.
Write the new word on the line.

1. farm + -er = __farmer__

2. act + -or = __actor__

3. sail + -or = __sailor__

4. teach + -er = __teacher__

5. visit + -or = __visitor__

6. play + -er = __player__

Directions Write the word from the box that best fits each definition.

__shipper__   **7.** one who ships packages

__inventor__   **8.** a person who makes new things

__teenager__   **9.** one between the ages of 13 and 19

| director |
| painter |
| shipper |
| teenager |
| inventor |
| writer |

__writer__   **10.** one who writes books

__painter__   **11.** an artist

__director__   **12.** a person who directs

© Pearson Education C

School + Home

Home Activity The activity uses words with the suffixes *-er* and *-or*. Work through the page with your child. Then work together to write definitions for the words in items 1–6.

Name_____

Draw Conclusions

A **conclusion** is a decision you reach after you think about details or facts in what you read and what you already know.

Directions Read the following passage. Then answer the questions.

If you could live anywhere, what place would you choose?

Would you choose a hot country? There is sunshine every day. You could play at the seashore and swim. You could fish in the lakes. You could plant crops that grow fast in the sunshine.

Would you choose a country where it is cold all the time? You could play in the snow. You could skate on the ice. You could use your sled to ride down the hills. You would have to keep on lots of clothes.

Or, would you choose the United States? You already know a lot about life in the United States because you live here!

1. Would a hot place be a good place for someone who likes to cook and eat outside? Why or why not?

A hot place would be good. Meals can be eaten outdoors.

2. Would a hot place be a good place for someone who likes to skate and ice-fish? Why or why not?

A hot place is not a good place to skate or ice-fish.

3. Would a very cold place be a good home for someone who likes to plant and grow crops? Why or why not?

Crops would not grow well in a very cold place.

4. Would a very cold place be a good home for someone who likes to swim outside? Why or why not?

A person cannot swim outside in a place where it is very cold.

5. Which place would you choose to live? Why?

Students' answers should include reasons for their choices.

Home Activity This activity asks questions about a story that requires drawing conclusions. Give your child a faulty conclusion, such as "I want some groceries, so I think I'll go to a movie." Ask your child to correct the sentence and give a reason.

© Pearson Education C

Name_____

Vocabulary

Directions Match each word from the box with its meaning.
Write the word on the line.

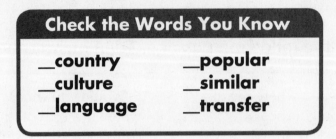

Check the Words You Know

__country __popular
__culture __similar
__language __transfer

__language__ **1.** the speech used by a group of people

__similar__ **2.** much the same

__country__ **3.** the land of a group of people

__popular__ **4.** liked by most people

__culture__ **5.** the customs of a group of people

__transfer__ **6.** to move from one place to another

Directions Write the word from the box that best completes each
question below.

7. What __language__ do they speak?

8. What is a __popular__ sport that everyone likes?

9. What __country__ do we live in?

10. Is Japan __similar__ to or different from the
United States?

© Pearson Education C

Home Activity The page helps your child read and write vocabulary. Work through the page with your
child. Then ask your child to write sentences using each of the vocabulary words.

Practice Book Unit 5

Name _____

Writing

Directions You need to decide what to write about. Read the questions below. Write answers to the questions to get ideas for your letter.

1. What is a new sport? _____ Letters should include a _____
2. What is a new kind of music? __ heading, greeting, the body, _____
3. What is a new game? _____ closing, and signature. The _____
4. What is a new kind of food? ___ content should be based on _____
5. What is a new clothing style? __ the answers to the questions. _____

Directions Fill in the blanks below with the words you will use for each part of your letter.

- The **heading** gives the reader your address. It also tells when you wrote the letter. What heading will you use in your letter?

  My street address: _____

  Today's date: _____

- The **greeting** opens the letter. It is a way to say "hello" to the person you are writing to. What greeting will you use in your letter?

  Dear _____ ,

- The **body** is the main part of the letter. (You'll write this later.)

- The **closing** ends the letter. It says "good-bye." You might close your letter by writing something like "Your pen pal." What closing will you use?

  _____

- The **signature** is your name. When writing to friends or family, use your first name. When writing to someone you don't know very well, you should use your full name. How will you sign your letter?

  _____

On another sheet of paper, write your letter. Be sure to include all the parts of a letter.

Home Activity This page helps your child write a letter to someone about something new in America. Help your child write a letter to a student in another country asking questions about the country's culture. The questions might be about sports, food, clothing, or music.

Vowel Sound in *ball*: *augh*, *ough*

Directions Circle the word with the vowel sound in **ball** to complete each sentence. Write the word on the line.

__thought__   **1.** Lu and I (decided/(thought)) we were different.

__caught__   **2.** He (threw/(caught)) baseballs with his left hand. I used my right.

__bought__   **3.** He ((bought)/wanted) rice. I chose cheese.

__daughter__   **4.** He was a son. I was a (girl/(daughter)).

__naughty__   **5.** He had a nice cat. My dog sometimes was ((naughty)/bad).

__sought__   **6.** He found books about space. I ((sought)/had) books about animals.

__taught__   **7.** His mother ((taught)/did) math. My mom was an artist.

__brought__   **8.** What ((brought)/kept) us together? Being best friends!

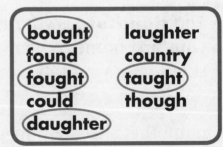

Directions First, circle the words that have the vowel sound you hear in **ball**. Then match each circled word to its clue. Write each word on the line.

__daughter__   **9.** a parent's female child

__fought__   **10.** what a boxer did

__bought__   **11.** paid for

__taught__   **12.** gave lessons

(bought)	laughter
found	country
(fought)	(taught)
could	though
(daughter)	

© Pearson Education C

Home Activity This page practices words with the vowel sound in *ball* spelled *augh*, *ough*. Challenge your child to name two words that rhyme with *bought* and are spelled *ough* (*brought, thought*) and a word that rhymes with *caught* and is spelled *augh* (*taught*).

Prefixes *over-*, *under-*, *out-*

Directions Add the prefix *over-*, *under-*, or *out-* to each base word.
Write the new word on the line.

1. over-   +   load   =   <u>overload</u>

2. out-   +   going   =   <u>outgoing</u>

3. under-   +   gone   =   <u>undergone</u>

4. over-   +   cooked =   <u>overcooked</u>

5. out-   +   field   =   <u>outfield</u>

6. under-   +   paid   =   <u>underpaid</u>

7. over-   +   due   =   <u>overdue</u>

8. out   +   line   =   <u>outline</u>

Directions Add the prefix *over-*, *under-*, or *out-* to the base word in ( )
to complete each sentence. Write the word on the line.

<u>outside</u>   **9.** When we lived in a hot country, I played (side)
every day.

<u>undergo</u>   **10.** My habits had to (go) a change when we
moved to a place where it rained a lot.

<u>overcoat</u>   **11.** During the winter, I have to wear an (coat).

<u>overjoyed</u>   **12.** I was (joyed) to find a friend who liked to
play chess!

Home Activity This activity works with words with the prefixes *over-*, *under-*, and *out-*. Work together to list other words with these prefixes. Use a dictionary for ideas.

© Pearson Education C

Name_____

Sequence

- The **sequence** of a story is the order in which events happen.
- **Clue words,** such as *first, next, then,* and *finally*, are often used to signal the sequence of events. Dates and times can also be clues. Sometimes, no clue words are used at all.

Directions Read the passage and use the information to complete the sequence chart below.

My family came to this country so my great-grandfather could find land to farm. The first part of their trip was on a big ship. It took many weeks to sail across the sea. They landed in New York. Then they rode on a train. Finally, they loaded their things on a wagon pulled by a team of horses. They rode on the wagon to their new home in the Northwest. Grandmother showed me pictures of the house and the barns they put up. It's the same house we live in today. I have the same address as my great-grandfather!

Directions Circle the statements in the boxes that best tell the beginning, middle, and end of the family's journey to America.

Beginning
1. They rode on a big ship.
   They rode on a train.
   They looked for a farm.

Middle
2. They didn't like New York
   They rode on a train.
   They rode on a ship.

End
3. They rode on a wagon to the Northwest.
   They rode on a big ship.
   They rode on a train.

4. Circle clue words in the passage that tell the order of events. Then write them on the line below.

first, then, finally

Home Activity The activity tells the order of events in a story. Find a short story. Read the story together and ask your child to tell what happened at the beginning, the middle, and the end of the story.

Name_____

Vocabulary

Directions Match each word with its definition. Write the word on the line.

__journey__ **1.** a long trip

__photograph__ **2.** a picture taken with a camera

__address__ **3.** place where one lives

__immigrant__ **4.** someone who comes to a country to live there

__apartment__ **5.** part of a large building where people live

__museum__ **6.** where sets of objects are kept and displayed

Directions Write a word from the box to complete each sentence below.

7. Ann made the long __journey__ across the sea.

8. She was an __immigrant__ , and she wanted to live in a new country.

9. She was very happy to find an __apartment__ for her family to live in.

10. She was proud to write her new __address__ on letters to send back home.

Write a Story

Write a story about how an immigrant might feel about coming to America to live. Use as many vocabulary words as possible.

© Pearson Education C

Home Activity This page helps your child read and write vocabulary words. Ask your child to tell you about a journey, a museum, or a photograph. Encourage your child to use the vocabulary words.

Name_____

Writing

Directions Circle the items you will use to draw a floor plan of an apartment.

markers   eraser   ink pen   paper

paste   pencils   photograph   ruler

Directions Decide the kind of apartment for which you will draw a floor plan. Put a checkmark beside your answers.

1. Whose apartment will you draw a floor plan for?

_____ a family of 1863   _____ a family of today

2. What rooms will be in the apartment?

_____ sitting room   _____ kitchen

_____ bathroom   _____ bedroom

_____ laundry room   _____ dining room

_____ TV room   _____ other rooms _____

3. How many rooms will be in the apartment?

_____ 3

_____ 4

_____ 5

_____ 6

_____ 7

On another sheet of paper, draw the floor plan of an apartment for a family you chose. Be sure to label each room.

The floor plan should be based on the choices selected, and the rooms should be labeled.

Home Activity This page helps your child draw a floor plan for an apartment. Help your child make a list of the rooms in your house or apartment and draw a floor plan for your home. Encourage your child to add any rooms he or she would like to have. Help your child label the rooms.

© Pearson Education C

Name_____

Long *i*: ind, ild; Long *o*: ost, old

Directions Circle the words in the poem with the long *i* sound and underline the words with the long *o* sound. Write each word on the lines.

At the Market

At the market, what can you (find?)
Peppers of every (kind,)
Hot ones and (mild) ones.
Red, orange, and <u>gold</u> ones.
Fat ones and thin ones.
There's some (wild)-looking ones!
<u>Sold</u> fresh in the morning,
They're sauce by evening!

Peppers For Sale

Long *i* words

1. __find__

2. __kind__

3. __mild__

4. __wild__

Long *o* words

5. __gold__

6. __sold__

Order of answers 1–4 and 5–6 will vary.

Directions Choose the words from the box that rhyme with each of the words below. Write the words from the box on the lines.

7. kind __grind__ __mind__

8. wild __child__ __mild__

9. sold __hold__ __told__

10. most __host__ __post__

child	hold	told
host	mild	mind
grind	post	

© Pearson Education C

Home Activity This page practices words with the long *i* sound as in *kind* and *child* and the long *o* sound as in *post* and *cold*. Challenge your child to name a single consonant that can be used to make words ending in *ind*, *ild*, *ost*, and *old*. (*mind, mild, most,* and *mold*)

Name_____

Suffixes -y, -ish

Directions Add the suffix **-y** or **-ish** to each word. Write the new word on the line.

1. speed + y = **speedy**
2. snow + y = **snowy**
3. fool + ish = **foolish**
4. child + ish = **childish**
5. meat + y = **meaty**
6. sleep + y = **sleepy**
7. hand + y = **handy**
8. yellow + ish = **yellowish**
9. boy + ish = **boyish**

Directions Separate each base word from the suffix and write each part on the lines.

10. **oil** + **y** = oily
11. **child** + **ish** = childish
12. **self** + **ish** = selfish
13. **crust** + **y** = crusty
14. **stick** + **y** = sticky
15. **girl** + **ish** = girlish

Home Activity This lesson uses base words and suffixes. Challenge your child to add suffixes to the base words *round, crunch, soap, green,* and *cloud* to make new words. *(roundish, crunchy, soapy, greenish,* and *cloudy)*

Name_____

Draw Conclusions

- A **conclusion** is a decision or opinion that makes sense based on facts and details.
- You can also use **what you already know** to **draw a conclusion.**

Directions Read the passage and use the information to complete the chart below.

> It's dinnertime, and I'm going to make French toast. I will try to make baked French toast. First, I'll put two thick slices of bread in milk and egg mixed together. Then, I'll put the soaked bread slices in a lightly greased baking pan. Next, I'll grind nutmeg for the top of each slice. And, finally, I'll bake it for 20 minutes. I'll serve it with butter and hot jam. It will make a great dinner.

Directions Answer the questions in boxes 1–4. Then write a conclusion about what you read.

1. Fact	2. Fact	3. Fact	4. What I Know
True or false? This dish will be baked.	What is soaked in milk and eggs?	What is used to make the toast taste good?	**Possible answer:** **I like French Toast.**
true	**bread**	**nutmeg, butter, jam**	

4. Conclusion

Answers may include that a traditional breakfast food can be served for dinner, that French toast can be baked as well as fried, or that the French toast is easy to make.

© Pearson Education C

Home Activity This activity works with drawing conclusions. Have your child tell you about something that happened to him or her at school. Then help your child summarize what happened and draw a conclusion from it.

Name_____

Vocabulary

Directions Match each word with its meaning. Draw a line to connect them.

1. delicious   a set of steps for cooking

2. ethnic   good to eat

3. recipe   a place to buy and eat a meal

4. restaurant   connected with a group of people

Directions Write the word from the box that best completes each sentence below.

5. At ___dinnertime___ , my family likes to eat a big meal.

6. Jim's family likes to go to a ___restaurant___ with many kinds of food.

7. They all like different ___ethnic___ foods.

8. Jim thinks that Indian food is the most ___delicious___ .

9. His likes a ___mixture___ of chicken and rice.

10. His mom asked for the ___recipe___ so she can make it at home.

Write a Recipe

On a separate sheet of paper, write a recipe for something you like to eat or drink. It can be something simple, such as a sandwich. Use as many vocabulary words as possible.

Recipes will vary.

© Pearson Education C

Home Activity This page helps your child read and write vocabulary words. Have your child plan a menu for dinner or help you prepare food from a written recipe. Encourage your child to use the vocabulary words in conversations.

Name_____

Writing

Directions Fill in the chart to create names for the items on a menu. Each word on a line should start with the same sound. The first one is done for you. **Answers should include names and adjectives.**

Person's Name	Adjective	Food
Tom's	Tasty	Tacos
		Dumplings
		Grapes
		Cake
		Soup
		Chicken

Directions Choose words from the following list to describe each dish. Circle the words you want to use.

chewy   delicious   select

chopped   golden   spicy

cold   great   stirred

cooked   green   sweet

dandy   simple

Word choices will vary.

Directions Make a list of other words you might use. Think about words that tell how the dish looks.

_____   _____

_____   _____

_____   _____

© Pearson Education C

Home Activity This page helps your child write names and descriptions of foods. Work through the page with your child. Talk with your child about the foods that members of your family enjoy eating. Then help your child write another description of a favorite dish.

Name_____

Syllables VCCCV

Directions Some words have three consonants in the middle, between two vowels: *monster, control.* Choose the word in ( ) with the VCCCV syllable pattern to finish each sentence. Write the word on the line.

pilgrim **1.** The (traveler, pilgrim) took a trip to another country.

hundred **2.** She went with a (hundred, thousand) other people.

complain **3.** The food was different, but she didn't (complain, argue).

surprises **4.** She thinks that (holidays, surprises) are fun!

instead **5.** She ate some dishes with lamb (instead, sometimes) of beef.

inspect **6.** She had a chance to (inspect, study) many old places.

Directions Circle the word in each group that has the VCCCV syllable pattern. Underline the letters that make the pattern.

7. human (par̲t̲n̲er) winner

8. (con̲s̲t̲ant) planet signal

9. forgive (mon̲s̲t̲er) wonder

10. (com̲p̲l̲ain) number writer

11. beyond robin (in̲s̲t̲ant)

12. chosen (con̲t̲r̲ol) copper

Home Activity This page practices words with syllables that include VCCCV. Work through the items with your child. Write these words: *children, hundred, monster.* Ask your child to say the words and underline the VCCCV pattern.

Practice Book Unit 5

© Pearson Education C

Name_____

Main Idea and Supporting Details

- The **main idea** is what a story is all about.

- **Details** are small pieces of information that help tell what a story is about.

- As you read, **ask yourself,** "What are the important ideas in the story so far."

- **Sum up** to help you understand what is happening.

Directions Read the following story.

Kendra saw all sorts of colorful rocks at the beach. She had been looking for something to collect. Kendra decided she would collect rocks.

Kendra loaded her backpack with red rocks and speckled rocks.

At home, Kendra looked for a place to keep her rocks. She found a pretty box. She put the rocks in the box and set it on the porch.

Kendra showed her rocks to everyone who came to visit.

Directions Complete the graphic organizer to tell what the story is all about. **Possible answers are shown.**

Supporting Details

1.
Kendra saw rocks at the beach.

2.
She collected red and speckled rocks.

3.
She put the rocks in a pretty box. She showed the rocks to everyone.

Main Idea

4. What the Story Is All About
how Kendra made a rock collection

Home Activity This page allows your child to find the main idea of a story. Work through the items with your child. Read a story with your child. Ask him or her to tell the main idea—what the story is all about.

Name_____

Vocabulary

Directions Draw a line from the word to its definition.

1. compare   to make or become better

2. hardship   as different as it can be

3. improve   to tell how things are alike

4. opposite   to set up a home in a new country or place

5. settle   something hard to put up with

6. surround   to shut in on all sides; enclose

> **Check the Words You Know**
>
> __compare
> __hardship
> __improve
> __opposite
> __settle
> __surround

Directions Fill in the blank with a word from the box that fits the meaning of the sentence.

7. He built a fence to ___surround___ the horses.

8. Reading books helps you ___improve___ your skills.

9. Some people decided to ___settle___ in the West.

10. It is a ___hardship___ to live without power.

11. You can ___compare___ kinds of cats to tell how they are alike.

12. Inside is the ___opposite___ of outside.

Write Questions

On a separate paper, write four questions you would like to ask a colonial boy or girl your own age. Use some vocabulary words.

Questions should express students' curiosity about these people of the past.

© Pearson Education C

Home Activity This page helps your child read and write vocabulary words. Work through the items with your child. Ask your child to tell two ways his or her life is different from that of a colonial child.

Name_____

Writing

Think about times in the past—even millions of years ago when there were dinosaurs! Choose a time.

Directions Circle any words from the box that you might use in your writing. Now answer these questions.

thrilling	games
creepy	food
hardship	school
power	chores
plumbing	boring
toys	

1. What time in the past did you choose?

<u>Choices will vary.</u>

2. What are some of your favorite things to do?

_____

_____

3. Could you do these things in the past? Explain.

<u>Students should tell why their activities could or could not be done</u>

<u>in the past.</u>

4. What could you do in the past that you can't do now?

<u>Students who would like to live in the past will likely stress the</u>

<u>excitement and overcoming challenges.</u>

5. What would be hard if you lived in the past? What would be fun?

<u>Students who would not like to live in the past probably will not</u>

<u>want to do without modern conveniences and technology.</u>

On another paper, write a paragraph telling if you would or would not like to live in the past. Explain your reasons.

Accept reasonable responses.

Home Activity This page helps your child write sentences about a topic. Work through the page with your child. Then have your child read the paragraph aloud.

© Pearson Education C

Name _____

Suffixes -hood, -ment

Directions Combine the base word and the suffix. Write the new word on the line.

1. pay + -ment = __payment__
2. boy + -hood = __boyhood__
3. excite + -ment = __excitement__
4. agree + -ment = __agreement__
5. child + -hood = __childhood__
6. move + -ment = __movement__
7. false + -hood = __falsehood__
8. neighbor + -hood = __neighborhood__

Directions Add **-hood** or **-ment** to the base word in ( ) to complete each sentence. Use the word box for help. Write the new word on the line.

| amazement |
| treatment |
| enjoyment |
| motherhood |

__enjoyment__ 9. The baby's (enjoy) of the toy made us smile.

__motherhood__ 10. Mrs. Brown enjoys (mother).

__treatment__ 11. The puppy grew fast with the good (treat).

__amazement__ 12. I was filled with (amaze) when I saw a rainbow.

© Pearson Education C

Home Activity This page practices words with the suffixes *-hood* and *-ment*. Work through the items with your child. Ask your child to name three things that cause him or her excitement.

Prefixes *pre-, mid-, post-*

Directions Add the prefix **pre-**, **mid-**, or **post-** to each base word. Write the new word on the line.

1. mid- + point = ___midpoint___

2. pre- + heat = ___preheat___

3. post- + war = ___postwar___

4. mid- + way = ___midway___

5. mid- + west = ___midwest___

6. pre- + teen = ___preteen___

7. post- + date = ___postdate___

8. pre- + view = ___preview___

Directions Choose the word from the box that best fits the definition. Write the word on the line.

midday
midweek
precook
prepay

___precook___ **9.** to cook something before

___midweek___ **10.** the middle of the week

___prepay___ **11.** to pay ahead of time

___midday___ **12.** the middle of the day

© Pearson Education C

School + Home **Home Activity** This page practices words with the prefixes *pre-*, *mid-*, and *post-*. Work through the items with your child. Ask your child to name a month in midsummer and to tell what time it is at midnight.

Name _____

Main Idea

- The **main idea** is what a passage is all about.
- **Details** are small pieces of information that tell about the main idea.

Directions Read the passage. Then answer the questions below.

> Long ago, people came to the United States from other countries. They came through Ellis Island. It is about a mile outside of New York City. It is named after Samuel Ellis who owned the island. He sold it to the state of New York.
>
> About 22 million people came through Ellis Island. They were given medical exams. A wall at Ellis Island has some of the people's names written on it. There is a Web site that has a list of people who came through Ellis Island.

1. What is the passage about? **Possible responses are given.**

__Ellis Island__

Give four details about Ellis Island.

2. __Ellis Island is named after Samuel Ellis.__

3. __Ellis Island is about one mile outside New York City.__

4. __About 22 million people came through Ellis Island.__

5. __There is a wall with people's names on it.__

6. Is the passage fiction or nonfiction? How do you know?

__The passage is nonfiction.__

__Student responses will vary.__

_____

Home Activity This page helps your child identify the main idea and details in a passage. Work through the items with your child. Talk with your child about people coming to the United States from other countries.

© Pearson Education C

Name _____

Vocabulary

Directions Fill in the word from the box that fits the meaning of the sentence.

1. An elephant is an ___enormous___ animal.

2. A heart is a ___symbol___ for love.

3. The statue in the town square is a ___monument___ to soldiers.

4. The soldiers fought for our country's ___liberty___ .

5. A ___sculptor___ carved the monument out of stone.

6. There is a statue of ___President___ Abraham Lincoln in Washington, D.C.

Check the Words You Know

__enormous
__liberty
__monument
__President
__sculptor
__symbol

Directions Draw a line from the word to its definition.

7. enormous — the leader of a country

8. liberty — freedom

9. monument — a person who carves or models figures

10. president — something set up to honor a person or an event

11. sculptor — something that stands for or represents something else

12. symbol — very, very large; huge

Write a Letter

On a separate paper, write a letter to the president of the United States. Write at least three sentences. Use as many of the vocabulary words as you can. **Sample sentences: My favorite symbol is the flag. Our school has an enormous one. Do you like being president?**

Home Activity This page helps your child read and write vocabulary words. Work through the items with your child. Then have your child tell what the vocabulary words in his or her letter mean.

© Pearson Education C

Name _____

Writing

• A **chart** can help you organize your ideas.

Directions Fill in the right side of the chart to tell about your school.

My School

Questions	Answers
What is the name of your school?	**Student responses will vary.**
Is the school named after a famous person? Who?	
What are the school colors?	
What is special about the school?	

Make a flag for your school. Answer these questions.

1. What shape will your flag be? _____

2. What colors will you use? _____

3. What people will you show? _____

4. What animals will you show? _____

On another paper, draw your flag. Write sentences to tell what the colors and symbols mean. Make sure your words are spelled correctly.

Students' flags will likely use the school colors. Other elements will vary according to the school.

© Pearson Education C

Home Activity This page helps your child design and describe a flag. Work through the page with your child. Then have your child read the description aloud.

Syllables V/V

Directions Circle the word with two vowels together that make two different sounds. Then underline the letters that stand for the two different sounds.

1. clean   paint   (pat**io**)

2. (med**ia**)   faith   search

3. greed   journal   (rod**eo**)

4. either   (cr**ue**l)   southern

5. beach   pound   (p**io**neer)

6. (d**ie**t)   poison   waiter

7. grain   group   (stad**iu**m)

8. ago   freeze   (ar**ea**s)

Directions Read the paragraph. Circle the underlined words that have two vowels together that make two different sounds. Write the words on the lines.

> **M**eg was eager to (create) a new song. She thought she had an (idea) for a tune. She tried it on the (piano.) Then she wrote a part for the (violin.) She liked the way it sounded.
>
> Meg invited two friends to go to the (studio) with her. Her friends were singers. Meg explained the music. The (trio) made a recording. Someday you might even hear it on the (radio)

9. __create__

10. __idea__

11. __piano__

12. __violin__

13. __studio__

14. __trio__

15. __radio__

© Pearson Education C

Home Activity This page practices words with syllables V/V. Work through the items with your child. Ask your child to read aloud the words he or she wrote on the page.

Name _____

Sequence

- **Sequence** is the order in which things happen in a story.
- **Clue words,** such as *before* and *after,* can tell you when something happens.

Directions Read the story. Then answer the questions below.

One morning, two bears woke up. They were hungry. The day before, they had eaten all the berries on their side of the river. "Look at those berries on the other side of the river," said Grizzly Bear. "If we jump up when the wind blows, we can catch a ride to our dinner."

Just then, a strong wind came up. The bears jumped into the air and were carried across the river. They landed among hundreds of berries. The bears ate enough to fill their bellies. After that, they felt sleepy. They took a long nap.

1. How did the bears feel when they first woke up?

The bears felt hungry.

2. What idea did Grizzly Bear have for getting food?

Jump up and let the wind blow them to the other side of the river.

3. What happened after Grizzly Bear told the other bear his idea?

A wind came up. The bears jumped into the air and were carried across the river.

4. How did the bears feel after they filled their bellies?

The bears felt sleepy.

5. What did the bears do last?

They took a long nap.

6. What clue words did you find in the story?

before, then, after

Home Activity This page helps your child identify the sequence of events in a story. Work through the items with your child. Read another story about animals with your child. Ask your child to tell what happened first, next, and last.

Vocabulary

Directions Choose the word from the box that matches each definition. Write the word on the line.

Check the Words You Know

__adopt
__capture
__comfort
__exercise
__provide
__struggle

__capture__ **1.** to make prisoner of; take by force

__provide__ **2.** to give what is needed or wanted; supply

__struggle__ **3.** to make great efforts with the body; try hard

__adopt__ **4.** to take for your own or as your own choice

__comfort__ **5.** ease; freedom from hardship

__exercise__ **6.** the active use of the body or mind for its improvement

Directions Circle the word at the end of each sentence that fits the meaning. Then write the word on the line to finish the sentence.

7. If you want a kitten, you can __adopt__ one from the animal shelter. (adopt) give

8. Animals need __exercise__ to stay healthy.   clothes (exercise)

9. A rabbit will __struggle__ if you pick it up. It doesn't like to be held. (struggle) bark

10. Food, water, and a place to live give most animals __comfort__ . sadness (comfort)

Write Sentences

On a separate paper, write three things wild horses need. Use complete sentences. Use as many vocabulary words as you can.

Responses will vary.

Home Activity This page helps your child read and write vocabulary words. Work through the items with your child. Ask your child to tell you why a wild horse would *not* make a good pet.

Name _____

Writing

Think about the wild animals in your neighborhood. Think about what can help them and hurt them. You will make a poster to tell other people.

Directions Circle any words from the box that you might use. Write other words you can use on your poster.

| healthy |
| safe |
| happy |
| hurt |
| free |
| wild |

1. <u>Responses for items 1–2 will vary.</u>

Now answer the questions.

2. What wild animals live near you?

_____

3. Do you think people should feed wild animals? Why or why not?

<u>Possible responses are given for questions 3–5.</u>

<u>People food is not good for wild animals.</u>

4. If someone puts poison in a garden to kill insects, what could happen to wild animals?

<u>If animals eat things from a garden, the poison could kill them.</u>

_____

5. If people leave trash, broken bottles, and old furniture outside, what could happen to wild animals?

<u>Animals can get hurt if they step on broken glass or trip over</u>

<u>furniture and other trash.</u>

Tape four papers together so you have a big poster. Write a title for your poster. List things people should and should not do to keep wild animals safe. You can draw pictures or paste pictures from magazines.

Students' posters should make the point that people need to be careful not to harm wild animals.

© Pearson Education C

Home Activity This page helps your child make a poster. Work through the page with your child. Have your child read the poster aloud.

Name _____

Common Syllables

Directions Read the passage. Circle each word that ends in **-tion**, **-sion**, or **-ture.** Then write each word in the correct column.

Summer vacation was filled with excitement. One day we went to see the sculpture garden in the park. Another time we watched some artists as they painted a giant mural. Each division of the mural showed a different time in our country's history. The last part showed the artist's vision for the future of our nation.

-tion	**-sion**	**-ture**
1. vacation	3. division	5. sculpture
2. nation	4. vision	6. future

Directions Choose the word from the box that finishes each word below. Two letters in each word are given. Write the other letters to complete the word.

7. d i r e c t i o n

8. f e a t u r e

9. m i s s i o n

10. a c t i o n

11. e x p r e s s i o n

12. c r e a t u r e

13. f u r n i t u r e

14. i m a g i n a t i o n

15. m a n s i o n

action
creature
direction
expression
feature
furniture
imagination
mansion
mission

© Pearson Education C

Home Activity This page practices words with the syllables *-tion, -sion,* and *-ture.* Work through the items with your child. Ask your child to write one sentence with the word *picture* and one with the word *question.*

Name _____

Multisyllabic Word Practice

Directions Underline the word in each sentence that has **three** syllables or parts. Then write the word on the line. Draw lines to divide the word into parts (example: un|der|line).

fur|ni|ture   **1.** I have a lot of <u>furniture</u> in my room: a bed, desk, chair, lamp, rug, and bookcase.

ex|pres|sion   **2.** The roaring lion had a scary <u>expression</u> on its face.

au|di|ence   **3.** The <u>audience</u> laughed when the actor fell off his chair.

en|ter|tain   **4.** A clown will <u>entertain</u> the children at the birthday party.

per|form|ance   **5.** The last <u>performance</u> of the movie is at nine o'clock.

tra|di|tion   **6.** A parade on Independence Day is a <u>tradition</u> in our town.

re|mem|ber   **7.** I must <u>remember</u> to study for the science test on Friday.

beau|ti|ful   **8.** The city looked <u>beautiful</u> after the big snowfall.

Directions Underline the word in each sentence that has **four** syllables and write the word on the line. Draw lines to divide the word into parts.

com|mu|ni|ty   **9.** In our <u>community</u>, people help their neighbors.

pre|sen|ta|tions   **10.** The judges made <u>presentations</u> for the prize cows at the fair.

© Pearson Education C

Home Activity This page practices words with three and four syllables. Work through the items with your child. Ask your child to say two sentences: one with the word *important* and one with the word *tomorrow*.

Compare and Contrast

- When you **compare and contrast,** you tell how things are alike and different.

- Look for **clue words** that signal comparisons and contrasts, such as *like, both, different,* and *however.*

- As you read, **ask yourself,** "How are these things alike? How are they different? What do I already know about these things?"

Directions Read the passage. Then answer the questions below.

Two big rivers in the world are the Nile and the Amazon. Both rivers are very long. However, the Amazon has more water flowing in it.

The Nile and the Amazon differ in another way. They are on two different continents. The Nile is in Africa. The Amazon is in South America.

There are many animals in both rivers. Crocodiles live in both the Amazon and the Nile. Unlike the Nile, the Amazon is home to one of the world's longest snakes, the anaconda.

1. What is one way the Amazon and Nile Rivers are alike?

Both are long rivers.

2. Are the Amazon and Nile located on different continents? What are the continents?

Yes. The Nile is in Africa. The Amazon is in South America.

3. What animal is found in the Amazon but not in the Nile?

anaconda

4. What is one animal that the Nile and Amazon have in common?

crocodile

5. How else might the Amazon and Nile rivers be alike?

Possible answers: Both rivers might have waterfalls. Both rivers might have fish. People might live near both rivers.

Home Activity This page helps your child compare and contrast. Work through the items with your child. Choose two things in your home, such as a table and a desk or a cat and a dog. Ask your child to tell how they are alike and different.

© Pearson Education C

Name _____

Vocabulary

Directions Choose the word from the box that matches each definition. Write the word on the line.

1. a way to show things __display__

2. to fill with a thought or feeling __inspire__

3. to cause to laugh or smile __amuse__

4. a place where plays are acted __theater__

5. to make a thing that has not been made before; cause to be __create__

6. to put into words __express__

<table>
<tr><td>Check the Words
You Know</td></tr>
<tr><td>__amuse
__create
__display
__express
__inspire
__theater</td></tr>
</table>

Directions Fill in the blank with a word from the box that fits the meaning of the sentence.

7. There is a __display__ of students' artwork in the hall.

8. Does the picture of a pig wearing a dress __amuse__ you?

9. Sam likes to __create__ pictures by pasting bottle tops on cardboard.

10. Artists __express__ their ideas in many different ways.

11. I like the posters that are outside the movie __theater__ .

12. Sometimes they __inspire__ me to see a certain movie.

Write an Ad

On a separate paper, write an ad for Pete's apple market. Make his apples sound yummy. Use as many of the vocabulary words as you can.

Sentences should describe different kinds of apples.

Home Activity This page helps your child read and write vocabulary words. Work through the items with your child. Ask your child to describe his or her favorite fruit.

© Pearson Education C

Name _____

Writing

Think about different ways to express yourself: art, acting, singing, dancing, writing. Think about how to describe the form of expression.

create	words
pretend	imagination
movement	express
draw	exciting
paint	thrilling

Students should describe their favorite way to express themselves and tell why they chose that form of expression.

1. What way to express yourself is your favorite?

_____

2. What do you like best about it?

_____

3. How does it make you feel?

_____

4. Do you like other people to watch as you do it or to look at it when it is finished? Why or why not?

_____

_____

5. Write a good sentence to begin your description.

_____

On another paper, write your description. You can use words from the box to help you. Make sure all your words are spelled correctly.

Home Activity This page helps your child write a description. Work through the page with your child. Then have your child read the description aloud.

© Pearson Education C

Name _____

Blending Multisyllabic Words

Directions Each word below has one or more word parts added to the beginning or the end of its base word. Underline the base word. Then write a sentence that uses the whole word. **Students' sentences will vary.**

1. un<u>reason</u>able _____

2. <u>care</u>fully _____

3. dis<u>agree</u>ment _____

4. re<u>appear</u>ed _____

5. un<u>prepare</u>d _____

6. <u>end</u>lessly _____

Directions Each base word below has a word part added to the beginning and end. Separate each base word from the other word parts and write each part on a line.

Base Word

7.	<u>dis</u>	+	<u>taste</u>	+	<u>ful</u>	=	distasteful
8.	<u>un</u>	+	<u>friend</u>	+	<u>ly</u>	=	unfriendly
9.	<u>un</u>	+	<u>plug[g]</u>	+	<u>ed</u>	=	unplugged
10.	<u>un</u>	+	<u>happy̶i</u>	+	<u>ly</u>	=	unhappily
11.	<u>un</u>	+	<u>law</u>	+	<u>ful</u>	=	unlawful
12.	<u>dis</u>	+	<u>honest</u>	+	<u>ly</u>	=	dishonestly
13.	<u>re</u>	+	<u>new</u>	+	<u>able</u>	=	renewable
14.	<u>re</u>	+	<u>fresh</u>	+	<u>ment</u>	=	refreshment
15.	<u>dis</u>	+	<u>trust</u>	+	<u>ful</u>	=	distrustful

© Pearson Education C

Home Activity This page practices words with prefixes and suffixes. Work through the items with your child. Ask your child how the base word *easy* changes when the suffix *-ly* is added.

Name _____

Main Idea

- The **main idea** is the most important idea in a passage. It tells what the passage is about.

- **Supporting details** are small pieces of information that tell about the main idea.

Some animals are born in unusual ways.

A frog begins as an egg. The egg hatches in about a week, and a small tadpole wiggles out. A tadpole looks a bit like a tiny fish. It swims around in water, looking for food to eat. As the tadpole eats, it grows and changes. It loses its tail and grows legs. Soon the tadpole is a frog.

A butterfly begins as an egg too. The egg hatches in a month, and out comes a caterpillar. A hard shell grows around the caterpillar. Inside the shell, the animal changes again. In about three weeks, out flies a butterfly!

Directions Read the passage. Then answer the questions below.

1. What is the main idea of the passage?

Some animals are born in unusual ways.

2. Give three details about a frog.

Any three: A frog begins as an egg. The egg hatches, and a tadpole wiggles out. The tadpole swims in water, looking for food to eat. It loses its tail and grows legs. It becomes a frog.

3. Give three details about a butterfly.

Any three: A butterfly begins as an egg. The egg hatches and becomes a caterpillar. A hard shell grows around the caterpillar. The caterpillar changes. It becomes a butterfly.

Home Activity This page helps your child identify the main idea and details in a passage. Work through the items with your child. Read a story with your child. Then ask your child to tell the main idea of the story.

© Pearson Education C

Name _____

Vocabulary

Directions Circle the word that completes each sentence. Then write the word on the line.

Check the Words You Know
_annoy   _disturb   _pollution
_cooperate   _intention   _require

1. Please be quiet and don't ___**disturb**___ me when I am studying.

    (disturb)   cooperate

2. The oil spill caused ___**pollution**___ in the ocean.

    intention   (pollution)

3. If we ___**cooperate**___ and work together, we can finish our project sooner.

    (cooperate)   annoy

4. Mosquito bites ___**annoy**___ me—they itch!

    require   (annoy)

Directions Choose a word from the box that matches each definition. Write the word on the line.

5. actions that make the environment dirty ___**pollution**___

6. to work together ___**cooperate**___

7. to need ___**require**___

8. a purpose; plan ___**intention**___

Write Laws

Write three silly laws. Write one law about pigs, one law about roller skating, and one law about hot dogs. Use as many of the vocabulary words as you can.

Responses will vary.

Home Activity This page helps your child read and write vocabulary words. Work through the items with your child. Make up a silly law for your child to follow. Ask him or her to make up a silly law for you to follow.

© Pearson Education C

Name _____

Writing

Think about what would make the world a better place. Think about what would make life more fun. Look at the words and phrases in the box for ideas.

1. What are three problems in the world that make you sad?

food	school
home	bedtime
healthy	pet
happy	television

Student responses will vary. Possible responses include pollution, harming trees, or unsafe places to play.

_____

2. How could someone fix those things?

Student responses will vary. Possible responses include picking up litter or encouraging others to recycle.

_____

3. What are three things you would *really* like to do or have?

Student responses will vary.

_____

_____

On another paper, write a law. For example, all children must have enough food to eat. Make sure all the words in your law are spelled correctly.

Student responses will vary.

Home Activity This page helps your child write a law. Work through the page with your child. Ask your child if being the person to fix a problem would be a hard job or an easy job and tell why.

© Pearson Education C

Name_____

Related Words

Directions Choose the word that best matches each clue. Write the word on the line.

1. coverings for the body   cloth   clothes   <u>**clothes**</u>

2. a person who plays sports   athlete   athletic   <u>**athlete**</u>

3. a person's handwritten name   sign   signature   <u>**signature**</u>

4. water in a tub for washing   bath   bathe   <u>**bath**</u>

5. the world of living things
   and the outdoors   natural   nature   <u>**nature**</u>

Directions The two related words in ( ) are missing from each sentence. Write the words in the correct places to complete each sentence.

6. The <u>**poet**</u> writes <u>**poetry**</u> that rhymes. (poet, poetry)

7. To <u>**define**</u> a word means to give its <u>**definition**</u> . (define, definition)

8. Hot <u>**volcanic**</u> ash came out of the <u>**volcano**</u> . (volcano, volcanic)

9. The <u>**pleasant**</u> weather <u>**pleased**</u> the campers. (pleased, pleasant)

10. I will <u>**decide**</u> what <u>**decision**</u> to make after I have heard all the facts. (decide, decision)

11. I enjoyed the <u>**performance**</u> because the <u>**performers**</u> were very good actors. (performers, performance)

12. To avoid <u>**repetition**</u> , don't <u>**repeat**</u> yourself. (repeat, repetition)

© Pearson Education C

Home Activity This page practices related words. Work through the items with your child. Ask your child to say or write a sentence that uses the words *please* (or *pleased*) and *pleasant*.

Name_____

Draw Conclusions

- A **conclusion** is a decision you reach based on what you read and what you know.
- Use **facts** and **details** to help you reach a conclusion.

Directions Read the passage. Then complete the chart below.

Sandy heard about the whales, so she hurried down to the bay. It was in the middle of a winter blizzard. Instead of swimming out to sea, whales had gone through the channel. Now the whales were stuck in ice.

People were helping the whales. Sandy helped chip ice to free them.

Firefighters brought hoses and other supplies. The tide was rising. Everyone waited to see what would happen.

The swish of water from the hoses sounded like a symphony. The water melted the ice. The whales wiggled loose.

1. Conclusion: What do you think happened to the whales?

The whales swam out to sea.

Details

2.
Sandy helped chip the ice.

3.
Firefighters brought hoses.

4.
The water melted the ice.

5.
The whales wiggled loose.

© Pearson Education C

Home Activity This page helps your child practice drawing conclusions. Work through the items with your child. Read part of a new story with your child. Stop and ask your child to draw a conclusion about the story.

Name_____

Vocabulary

Directions Solve each riddle using a word from the box. Write the word on the line.

1. I am a kind of writing that might rhyme.

What am I? __poetry__

2. I am the regular repetition of a beat.

What am I? __rhythm__

3. I am a strong feeling.

What am I? __emotion__

4. I am another word for soft or thin.

What am I? __delicate__

5. I am another word for say.

What am I? __recite__

Directions Read each sentence. Circle the underlined word that makes sense.

6. I will (compose)/invite a poem about a mouse who lives in a house.

7. The mouse is sad and is full of rhythm/(emotion).

8. The tiny mouse is (delicate)/poetry, with soft fur.

9. The mouse likes to jump when I play music—she has emotion/(rhythm).

10. I will (recite)/compose my poem aloud to my class.

Write a Poem   Accept rhyming poems about cats.

On a separate paper, write a poem about a cat. Your poem should be at least four lines long. Use rhyming words (such as *bat, fat, hat, mat*). Try to use vocabulary words too.

© Pearson Education C

Home Activity This page helps your child read and write vocabulary words. Work through the items with your child. Ask your child to read his or her poem to you.

Name_____

Writing

Think about different ways you could perform a poem for an audience if you were shy. Check off good ideas in the box.

> __sing   __write it and hold it up
> __act it out   __use a different kind of voice
> __wear a mask or costume   __work with a friend

1. How would you perform your poem?   **Responses will vary.**

_____

2. Why would you perform it this way?

_____

_____

3. What supplies do you need?

_____

4. What help do you need from other people?

Possible response: I would practice performing my poem for a close

friend or family member first.

5. Write a good sentence to begin your description. Start by telling what you would do.

_____

_____

© Pearson Education C

On a separate paper, describe how you would perform your poem and why you chose that way. Be sure all your words are spelled correctly.
Students should describe their choice and why it would help a shy person.

Home Activity This page helps your child write a description. Work through the page with your child. Ask your child if he or she thinks the audience would like this kind of poetry performance and why.

Name _____

Words for Writing and Reading

_____   _____

_____   _____

_____   _____

_____   _____

_____   _____

_____   _____

_____   _____

_____   _____

_____   _____

_____   _____

_____   _____

_____   _____

_____   _____

_____   _____

_____   _____

_____   _____

Words for Writing and Reading

_____   _____

_____   _____

_____   _____

_____   _____

_____   _____

_____   _____

_____   _____

_____   _____

_____   _____

_____   _____

_____   _____

_____   _____

_____   _____

_____   _____

_____   _____

_____   _____

_____   _____

Name _____

Reading Log

Date	What is the title?	Who is the author?	What did you think of it?

Name _____

Reading Log

Date	What is the title?	Who is the author?	What did you think of it?

Name ______________________

Reading Log

Date	What is the title?	Who is the author?	What did you think of it?

Name _____

Reading Log

Date	What is the title?	Who is the author?	What did you think of it?

Practice Book

Name _____

Reading Log

Date	What is the title?	Who is the author?	What did you think of it?